UNIVERSITY OF OXF
ASHMOLEAN MUSE

ANCIENT EGYPT

BY
P. R. S. MOOREY
(2nd Revised edition)

ASHMOLEAN MUSEUM, OXFORD
1992

ASHMOLEAN MUSEUM PUBLICATIONS ON MIDDLE AND
FAR EASTERN ART AND ARCHAEOLOGY:

First published 1970
Revised edition published 1983 [ISBN 0 900 9087 9]

This further revised edition published 1988, reprinted with
additional colour plates and minor corrections 1992.

ISBN 0 907849 76 8

Cover: Pottery lion seated on a plinth, found with a cache of
royal sculpture within the temple precinct at Hierakonpolis;
late Protodynastic — end of the Old Kingdom (c. 2700-2200
B.C.). (Ht. 42.4 cm; E. 189).
Photograph by Werner Forman.

Designed by Andrew Ivett
Printed and bound in Great Britain by Henry Ling & Co Ltd.

Introduction

Egypt's Legacy and the Development of Egyptology

It has been the peculiar fate of ancient Egypt to be represented in the popular imagination of the western world, from the Ancient Greeks onwards, by a series of misinterpreted images and symbols or wholly untypical personalities. Today the pathological and religious vagaries of the 'heretic' Pharaoh Akhenaten, the famous painted limestone head of his queen Nefertiti, the tomb of Tutankhamun, not to mention the lovelife of Cleopatra, serve all too often to epitomize the glory that was pharaonic Egypt. The familiar mummy, when not the major prop of horror films, symbolizes a way of life which it seemed cared only for pomp and splendour in death. The growth of this myth is as fascinating as it is instructive.

Some centuries before the Greeks wrote their first descriptions of Egypt in the fifth century B.C., Egyptian architectural forms and artistic motifs had already permeated the arts of Phoenicia and the Levant where they were freely and extravagantly used in metalwork, carved ivories (see Near Eastern Gallery display), seals and jewellery. Already it was the outward appearance, not the essence of Egyptian art, which was imitated, often to the point of parody. The effect of such artistic licence was negligible compared with the profound and enduring effect of a fundamental misconception of Egyptian culture bequeathed to the west by Graeco-Roman scholars.

Few of the most influential could speak Egyptian and virtually none had a first-hand knowledge of the hieroglyphic script. Instead of understanding the phonetic function of the signs—in simplest terms their use as 'letters'—they regarded the hieroglyphs as metaphorical and symbolic, erecting an enormous edifice of learning on the totally false assumption that each sign had a complex allegorical significance. As a direct result Egypt became renowned and highly esteemed in the Roman Empire as a source of occult learning and magic. It was a strange quirk of fate which, at a crucial moment in the intellectual history of western Europe, brought to the surface after almost a thousand years of oblivion the very book which best epitomized this interpretation of Egypt's legacy. In about 1419 a Florentine traveller, Christoforo Buondelmonti, found on the Greek island of Andros a manuscript of the *Hieroglyphica* of Horapollo, written about the fourth century A.D., and in 1422 took it back with him to Florence, where it was rapidly copied and circulated. Its erroneous interpretation of Egyptian hieroglyphs became not only the cornerstone of Renaissance Egyptology, but for the next four centuries the virtually unchallenged authority on all hieroglyphic questions.

This bastard literary tradition was to some extent matched by an equally misconceived artistic one. From the fall of the Roman Empire until well into the seventeenth century the artistic achievement of Egypt was represented in Europe by antiquities preserved in the ruins of ancient Rome and Hadrian's villa at Tivoli. These, when genuine, were normally the work of Egyptian sculptors after *c*. 600 B.C., but more often pastiches or fresh creations in the Egyptian manner by Roman sculptors. Artistically the most influential of all 'Egyptian' statues were those ordered by the Emperor Hadrian to commemorate his favourite Antinous, who had committed suicide by drowning himself in the Nile in A.D. 130. Even the most prominent of surviving genuine Egyptian antiquities, the numerous obelisks brought to Rome by emperors from Augustus onwards, were compromised by the existence of examples with imitation hieroglyphic inscriptions produced in Rome to satisfy imperial taste when the supply from Egypt had been exhausted.

The seventeenth century brought a marked change. Though it was two more centuries before the myth of the hieroglyphs was exposed, a growing flow of antiquities and information from Egypt slowly paved the way for a more realistic view of its ancient civilization. Oxford was among the first universities to have its own collection of Egyptian antiquities, thanks to the generosity of men like Archbishop Laud (*pl.* 1), the merchant Aaron Goodyear and the Rev. Robert Huntington (*pl.* 2). Some of their gifts were used in the eighteenth century to illustrate an essay on hieroglyphs by the Scottish author and traveller, Alexander Gordon (1737), and in 1763 they appeared in *Marmora Oxoniensia*.

In the eighteenth century three works, Montfaucon's *L'Antiquité expliquée et représentée en figures*, 1719-24, the monumental *Recueil d'antiquitiés egyptiennes . . .*, 1752-64 of the Comte de Caylus, and Georg Zoega's remarkable, and still indispensable, *De origine et usu obeliscorum*, 1797, took Egyptological studies about as far as they could go without a true appreciation of the hieroglyphic script, whilst providing artists in many fields with stimulating pattern books. In Oxford during the eighteenth and early nineteenth century the Egyptian collections slowly grew, fed by gifts from travellers and scholars whose urge to collect the exotic and curious in whatever form was singularly well satisfied by the still mysterious artefacts of ancient Egypt. The last, and most outstanding, of these scholars was the Rev. G. J. Chester (1831-92), a very shrewd and skilful buyer of antiquities, who added many hundreds of objects to the collections between 1865 and his death. In 1881 he published a catalogue of the Ashmolean's Egyptian

1. Shawabtis presented to the Bodleian Library, Oxford, in 1635 by Archbishop Laud: *left*, green-glazed shawabti of Tentrudj, daughter of Tentamun, Late Period; *right*: green stone shawabti with a pseudo-hieroglyphic inscription on the back, post-Pharaonic. (Hts. 14.3 cm, 6.5 cm).

collection, then so very much his creation. In effect it marked the end of an era.

It was a chance discovery in 1798 during Napoleon's invasion of Egypt of a bilingual inscription at Rashid-Rosetta in the western delta which at a single stroke led to the transformation of western knowledge of ancient Egypt. This inscription, now in the British Museum, bears a copy of a decree issued in 196 B.C. in Memphis by an assembly of Egyptian priests in honour of King Ptolemy V Epiphanes (203-181 B.C.), written first in Egyptian hieroglyphic script, then in demotic and then in Greek. The Greek text was rapidly translated and in the next twenty years a number of scholars including the Swedish diplomat Akerblad (1763-1819) and the English scientist Young (1773-1829) made vital contributions to unravelling the Egyptian text. But it was the French scholar, J.F. Champollion (1790-1832), whose profound knowledge of Coptic (see p. 38) and brilliant analysis of the inscription enabled him first in the epoch-making *Lettre à M. Dacier* of 1822 and then in his *Précis du système hiéroglyphique* of 1824 to formulate the system of grammar and general decipherment upon which all subsequent Egyptology is based. In the next fifty years industrious expeditions copied an enormous number of visible inscriptions and numerous antiquities were looted from Egypt to swell museum collections in Europe. In the second half of the nineteenth century Egyptology was established as a disciplined and scientific field of study. The Frenchman August Mariette (1821-81) laid the foundations of the Egyptian Antiquities Service, created a National Museum of Antiquities and strove to control the wholesale expropriation of antiquities. The Germans Karl Brugsch (1827-94) and Adolf Erman (1854-1937) pioneered the systematic study of the Egyptian language and the Englishman W.M.F. Petrie (1853-1942) founded Egyptian archaeology on firm principles of accurate observation, precise recording and rapid publication.

In the years following 1884 regular allocations from Petrie's excavations, and those of his associates, transformed the Ashmolean Museum's Egyptian Department from a random miscellany of objects into a collection of true historical interest.

The Geographical Background

Egypt is defined here, in terms an ancient Egyptian would have understood, as the cultivated valley of the river Nile extending northwards from the great granite cataract across the river near modern Aswan, first through sandstone, then through limestone deposits, whence it fans out into the delta (*fig. 1*). The river covers about 750 miles in its course from Aswan to the Mediterranean. The width of arable land on either bank varies from one to twenty-four miles in the valley, finally expanding to 125 miles in the broadest part

of the delta. Before the recent creation of 'Lake Nasser' in Nubia the fertility of this narrow corridor of land, hemmed in by desert, rested entirely upon the Nile's annual inundation. Though this varied greatly in size, it generally renewed the surface of the land with a rich deposit of alluvium. Normally the river was at its lowest in May; then, as rains in central Africa and melting snow and rains in the Abyssinian highlands increased, the flow of water rose to a peak-level in October. The ancient Egyptians controlled and used the flood by building dykes and basins, digging irrigation canals, sinking wells and using the *shadūf*, a water-raising device, to irrigate gardens. The maintenance of these vital constructions and the organization of ploughing, sowing and reaping in the appropriate seasons were carefully and systematically organized from earliest times. The legend of the seven lean years and the seven years of plenty was not a fantasy; it was always a haunting possibility (*pl. 3*).

The immemorial contrast between the rich earth of the valley and the arid expanse of its desert frame was

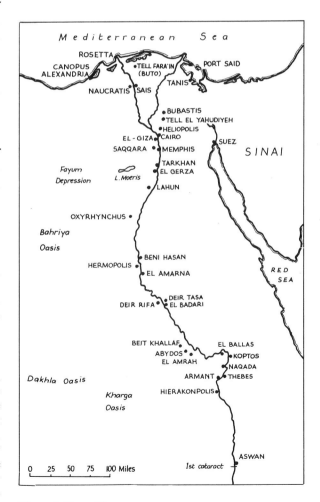

Figure 1. Map of Egypt.

epitomized by the ancient Egyptians in calling their homeland *Kēme(t)* ('the Black') in contrast to *Deshre(t)* ('the Red'). The Greek name we use, *Aigyptos*, is thought to derive from an Egyptian epithet for Memphis, capital during the Old Kingdom, which meant 'Home of the Spirit of Ptah'.

In almost every respect Egypt was self-sufficient. Agriculturally the land was exceptionally rich; animals, birds and fish were abundant. Save for timber, regularly obtained by sea from the Lebanon, all the basic raw materials for Egyptian craftsmen were to hand. Trade was stimulated not so much by necessity as by the growing demands of a highly civilized society for luxury goods like silver and lapis-lazuli from Western Asia, and incense, sandalwood, ivory and exotic animals from Punt, somewhere on the coast of modern Somaliland.

The valley itself had two strongly contrasted geographical divisions which were reflected in administrative practice and always underlay the political structure of Egypt:

1. *Upper, or southern, Egypt (Shemau)* ran from just north of the First Cataract at Aswan to a point never precisely determined (now at Cairo). It was divided into twenty-two *nomes* (districts) for administrative purposes. This part of Egypt was represented among royal insignia by the White Crown (*pl.* 7). Its symbol was a plant which is probably the flowering *scirpus*-reed or sedge and its titulary deity the vulture goddess Nekhbet of el-Kab, a city near the ancient capital of *Nhn* (Hierakonpolis).

2. *Lower, or northern, Egypt (To-mehu)* largely comprised the delta divided into twenty nomes. This region was represented by the Red Crown (*pl.* 6), and the bee; its titulary deity was the cobra-goddess Wadjet (Edjo) of the city *Dp*, near the ancient capital of *Pe*.

Egypt is physically isolated by four peripheral regions:

1. *The Western or Libyan Desert* is a desolate, rocky area devoid of natural resources and with few important oases. It was little used by the ancient Egyptians save for transit to the Sudan or coastal Libya.

2. *The Eastern Desert*, leading to the Red Sea, is a mountainous region of isolated, widely scattered wells, very rich in minerals and hard stones which the Egyptians exploited from earliest times.

3. *The Sinai Peninsula*, source of turquoise and copper, was a frontier region, vital to the defence of the country against intruders from Western Asia.

In all these directions land communications generally meant between five and eight days of desert caravanning.

4. *Nubia*, lying between the First and Third Cataracts, was the gateway to the riches of Equatorial Africa, a valuable source of gold and a buffer region against intruders from the south. The land itself is inhospitable. The desert cliffs cut in very close to the river reducing arable land to isolated patches and the Second and Third Cataracts are serious obstacles to movement by river (see also p. 58, *fig* 3).

2. Limestone cornice of a false door, from a *mastaba*-tomb at Saqqara—one of three antiquities acquired in Egypt in the 1670's by the Rev. Robert Huntington and presented by him to the University in 1683. The tomb owner Shery, a high official of Dynasty IV, and his wife Khentetka are shown beside a table loaded with food offerings. (0.44 × 1.06 m; 1836.479).

Physical isolation and economic self-sufficiency had profound effects on the development of Egyptian civilization. Although there were times, increasingly after *c*. 1000 B.C., when enemies crossed the barriers of sea and desert to invade Egypt, and places, particularly the eastern delta and Nubia, where foreigners infiltrated into the country, they had little cultural influence. Commercial and diplomatic relations with Western Asia extended back to predynastic times, and foreign artefacts entered Egypt regularly, but whereas Egyptian cultural influence was pronounced in Phoenicia, there was virtually no reciprocal influence in Egypt. The distinctive character of Egyptian civilization which emerged in the early third millennium B.C. survived right through until the spread of Christianity. This is not to say it was static. It was subject to growth and change like any thriving society, but it was a gradual process within a fixed intellectual and artistic framework which was regularly modified, but never fundamentally changed.

Geographical factors have also controlled the survival of archaeological evidence in Egypt. In Upper Egypt where the desert is close and arable land precious the dead were always buried in the dry desert sands, which have preserved them exceptionally well, whilst the great temples and royal tombs were set at the foot of the rocky scarps of the valley where they have survived, albeit battered. As a direct result we know far more of Egyptian funerary customs and temple architecture than we do of towns and villages. The ancient Egyptians had an acute awareness of life after death, but it must be remembered that the nature of the available evidence may greatly exaggerate this. The continuing density of settlement, the constant deposit of river mud and natural forces of destruction have left little or no trace in the valley of human settlements like those commonly encountered in other Near Eastern countries. Nor does the delta provide evidence to restore the balance, for there moisture and alluvial deposit have wrought an even greater destruction, all too often obliterating cities and temples which might have yielded vivid witness of Egypt's relations with Western Asia and the Mediterranean world. In one important respect Egyptian archaeology is particularly fortunate. The preservation of inscriptions on stone, wood, bone and papyrus, of richly decorated and lavishly furnished tombs, and the survival of written evidence in Classical and Coptic sources has permitted a much fuller understanding of ancient Egyptian civilization than is yet possible in less favoured, if equally literate, ancient civilizations.

Chronology

Predynastic Egypt

For the period before the use of written records,

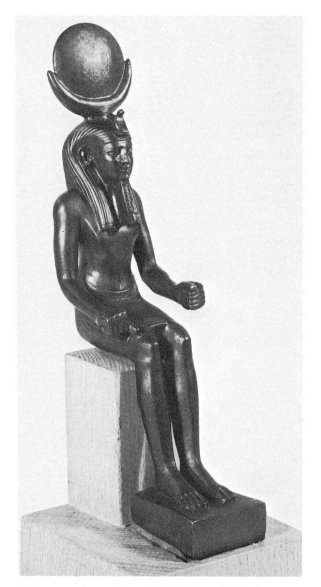

3. Bronze statuette of the god Osiris-Lunus, believed to influence the risings of the Nile; Late Period.
(Ht. 17 cm; Queen's College Loan 1089).

scholars have devised a relative chronology based entirely on archaeological evidence. Elsewhere in Western Asia prehistoric chronology is largely based on the analysis of the layers of debris from successive settlements in one place (stratigraphy) which have formed a mound or *tell*. These are virtually absent in Egypt. At the very end of the nineteenth century Petrie was thus forced to evolve a relative chronology based not on stratigraphy, but on a comparative study of the pottery he found in a number of cemeteries of the predynastic period, notably at Naqada, Abadiya and Hu (*pl.* 4). He studied the association of various types of pottery in grave-groups statistically and deduced fifty-one consecutive stages of development numbered 30-80, leaving 1-29 for subsequent discovery of earlier objects. These stages he called 'Sequence Dates' (S.D). It is important to remember that this is merely a convention which assumes neither a correspondence to absolute dates nor that the steps are of equal length. At first Petrie divided the series into two, later three, main groups or cultures, named after villages nearest to the relevant cemetery: *Amratian* (S.D. 30-37), *Gerzean* (S.D. 38-61) and *Semainian* (S.D. 61-78). The last period is now taken to overlap with Dynasties I-II after *c.* 3000 B.C. Some scholars refer to the two main pre-dynastic phases as Naqada I (*c.* S.D. 30-38) and II (S.D. 39-63) after the largest cemetery Petrie excavated, with a final phase, Naqada III, covering the emergence of a united Egypt. An earlier period *Badarian* was recognized in subsequent excavations at el-Badari. Rather meagre stratigraphy in a settlement at Hammamiya has confirmed the general validity of the S.D. system.

Pharaonic or Dynastic Egypt

The word 'pharaoh' used to refer to the rulers of ancient Egypt reached us directly through the Old Testament. The Egyptian 'per-'o' originally referred not to the man but to his palace ('Great House'). Only after *c.* 1400 B.C. did it come to apply to the ruler himself as in the biblical account of Joseph and Moses. The fully developed ancient name of each pharaoh may appear very complex until it is realized that most of it consists of titles and epithets common to each ruler. The crucial elements in the name are those two invariably written in a *cartouche* (frame), symbolizing the pharaoh's power over all 'which is encircled by the sun'. Of these the first (*prenomen*) is preceded by the

4. Pottery with incised and painted decoration, from a Predynastic burial at Naqada; Naqada I period (S.D. 32), c. 4500-4000 B.C. (Hts. 20 cm, 5.5 cm, 22 cm; 1895.317, 491 and 470, from grave 1823).

Concise Chronological Table

Absolute dates before 3000 B.C. are very approximate;
see pp. 7 ff. for discussion of chronological problems.

PERIOD	DYNASTY	DATE
Badarian	—	Before *c.* 4000 B.C.
Naqada I (Amratian)	—	*c.* 4000 - 3500 B.C.
Naqada II (Gerzean)	—	*c.* 3500 - 3000 B.C.
Naqada III	—	*c.* 3000 - 2920 B.C.
Protodynastic	Dynasties I - II	*c.* 2920 - 2649 B.C.
Old Kingdom	Dynasties III - VI	*c.* 2649 - 2150 B.C.
First Intermediate	Dynasties VII - X	*c.* 2150 - 2040 B.C.
Middle Kingdom	Dynasties XI - XII	*c.* 2134 - 1783 B.C
Second Intermediate	Dynasties XIII - XVII	*c.* 1783 - 1550 B.C.
New Kingdom	Dynasties VXIII - XX including the 'Amarna Period'	*c.* 1550 - 1070 B.C.
Late Period	Dynasties XXI - XXXI including: XXV: Nubian Dynasty XXVI: Saïte Dynasty XXVII: First Persian Occupation	*c.* 1070 - 333 B.C.
Ptolemaic Period		332 - 30 B.C.
Roman and Byzantine Period		30 B.C. - A.D. 641
Islamic Conquest		A.D. 641

---

title 'he who belongs to the sedge and the bee', or more prosaically, 'King of Upper and Lower Egypt' and is almost always compounded with the name of the sun-god Rē. The second (*nomen*) introduced by the epithet 'son of Rē', was usually the name borne by the king before his accession. It is this name, commonly in its Greek form, by which each pharaoh is now known. Thus Thutmose (Greek: Tuthmosis) III bore the names: *Menkheperrē Dhutmose*. Under the earliest dynasties each separate year was named after a conspicuous event; but by the Middle Kingdom the Egyptians regularly dated their inscriptions by the year of the pharaoh's reign: "year 4, second month of the inundation (see below), day one under the Majesty of King x." No continuous era was over used in the Pharaonic period.

The study of mathematics and astronomy began in pre-dynastic times, long before the earliest surviving documents relating to them were written. Thus the origins of the Egyptian calendar remain unknown. In the Pharaonic period the year was divided into 12 months of 30 days each (i.e. three 10 day weeks), completed to 365 days by addition of five "added" days. Each year was divided into the three seasons of inundation, winter and summer, each four months long. But, since the Egyptians never used the device of adding an extra day every four years (our leap year), to bring the civil year of 365 days into line with the astronomical year of approximately 365¼ days, the situation of the seasons in relation to the months was mobile. In about 120 years the civil year would be a whole month in advance of the astronomical year; in about 1460 years any given astronomical event would have fallen in turn on every different day of the civil year.

At some point in the remote past the Egyptians had recognized that the Nile began to rise again about the same time each year (mid. July in our calendar), when the dog-star Sirius was first to be seen again shortly before sunrise after being invisible for a long period (heliacal rising of Sirius). This came to be regarded as New Year's Day: "first month of inundation, day 1". Now, if this had always been the start of the Egyptian civil year, the seasons would have run as follows: inundation (mid. July to mid. November), winter (mid. November to mid. March), summer (mid. March to mid. July). But, because the Egyptians failed to adjust their civil calendar, the real summer might fall in the winter of the civil calendar and *vice versa*. As it is recorded that the civil New Year's Day and the heliacal rising of Sirius coincided in A.D. 139, it may be calculated exactly when this had previously occurred, since, as has been noted, it was a cyclical recurrence at approximately every 1460 years (the "Sothic Cycle"). It was not until the Persian period that the twelve months received names derived from certain feasts; before that they were numbered, as in the case cited above, and allotted to one or other of the three seasons.

The Egyptians divided the day into 24 hours, 12 to the day, 12 to the night; for religious and astronomical purposes they had their own names, but in everyday language, since the means for measuring hours were imprecise, they spoke of 'in the morning' or 'at time of night'. Both water-clocks (*clepsydrae*) and shadow-clocks were used to measure the hours.

The chronological system adopted by Egyptologists for the historical period from *c.* 3000 B.C. is based on the arrangements of rulers into approximate family groups, known as *dynasties*, used by the Graeco-Egyptian priest Manetho in preparing a history of Egypt in the early third century B.C. His dynastic lists have come down to us in the abridged versions of the Christian historians Africanus (early third century A.D.), Eusebius (early fourth century A.D.) and a much later compiler, known as Syncellus (*c.* A.D. 800); other parts of Manetho's history are preserved in the work of the Jewish historian Josephus (first century A.D.). Of the ancient Egyptian sources used by Manetho virtually nothing has survived. Only two documents: the 'Royal Canon' of Turin compiled in the reign of Ramesses II (*c.* 1290-1224 B.C.) and the

much earlier 'Palermo Stone' and its related fragments, inscribed during Dynasty V (*c.* 2465-2323 B.C.) illustrate the kind of ancient annals he might have used. Three other lists, of kings' names only, inscribed on monuments at Abydos, Saqqara and Karnak during the New Kingdom, though selective, provide valuable comparative evidence. These may be supplemented in some cases by contemporary records, by biographical inscriptions, by the diplomatic correspondence of the fourteenth century B.C. from el-Amarna, the annals of Thutmose III (*c.* 1479-1425 B.C.) and literary works with relevant historical information.

These lists provide only a relative chronology; the establishment of an absolute chronology in terms of regnal years is much more difficult. Although some early records give the length of reigns, the uneven character of the surviving evidence and the possibility of partly contemporaneous, rather than consecutive, dynasties means that the reliability of dates before the New Kingdom varies considerably. Most twelfth dynasty dates are fixed within a margin of two or three decades; but the start of Dynasty I may be wrong by as much as 150 years either way. Even in the new Kingdom there is still a margin of error of at least a decade or so. From Dynasty XII (*c.* 1991-1783 B.C.) onwards records of a number of lunar dates and observations of the rising of the star Sothis in conjunction with the sun have survived. Though even this evidence is by no means conclusive, it does allow, by providing reasonably fixed points, for more certainty in dating reigns during the next thousand years. In the Late Period historical and biographical inscriptions relating to the cult of the Apis bulls at Memphis give fixed points and a basis for chronology, which achieves precision from about 664 B.C. Synchronisms with other Western Asiatic and Mediterranean countries in the later Graeco-Roman period play an important part in determining Egyption chronology.

For general convenience modern scholars have grouped Manetho's dynasties into blocks: Old Kingdom, Middle Kingdom, New Kingdom and Late Period. The intervals of anarchy, foreign invasion and general political disruption are arbitrarily termed 'Intermediate Periods'. It is during these periods that the overlapping of dynasties provides particular chronological difficulties and it may turn out that they are considerably shorter than is currently assumed.

In recent years the Carbon-14 method of determining absolute dates has been applied to Egyptian material. The margin of error in the method is still too great for it to offer a significant contribution for periods where the historical evidence is relatively well-ordered; but for the early historic and prehistoric periods it is increasingly useful, providing the basis for the dating given on p. 9 for these periods.

1. Prehistory and History to A.D. 641

The Prehistoric Period

Men first penetrated the Nile Valley as nomadic hunting communities during the *Palaeolithic* Period (*c.* 700,000-7000 B.C.). In the Ashmolean's displays they are represented by a few stone tools from gravels of a former bed of the River Nile, near Thebes, representing hundreds of thousands of years of human activity in the area. By the end of this extremely long phase, that is by about 7000 B.C., seasonal camp sites may be traced at sites like El Kab, exploiting the wide variety of fish to be caught in the Nile and using the carefully made, and minutely retouched, flint blades and microblades taken to distinguish human activity in the *Epipalaeolithic* Period.

Already five thousand years earlier the use of cereals, in association with grinding stones and what may be sickle blades, is evident on various sites in the Nile Valley. But it was not until after about 6000 B.C. that controlled agriculture and husbandry in larger and more permanent settlements slowly became standard. It is still not entirely clear whether this was largely an indigenous development or whether the relatively rapid diffusion of the new agricultural way of life in Egypt resulted in some way from external stimuli and, if so, whether through overland contacts with the Sahara or with the Levant. The course of such developments is still much better known in Upper than in Lower Egypt, which will be considered here briefly before the classic Upper Egyptian sequence, established by Petrie. This is very well illustrated in the Ashmolean displays.

The earliest known farming community in Lower Egypt is that at Merimde in the western Delta, occupied in the first half of the fifth millennium B.C. by

5. Later Predynastic pottery decorated in red with scenes on the Nile including figures, boats, marsh birds and antelope; the tall jar is painted with spots, to resemble patterned stone, but the shape imitates the "wavy-handled jars", first imported from Palestine but then widely copied in Egypt at this period. Naqada II period (S.D. 46-52), c. 4000-3000 B.C.
(*Left to right*: hts. 20, 8.9, 18.8, 10.2 cm; 1895.568, 606 and 571, from graves at Naqada; E.2823, from Abadiya, cemetery B).

people familiar with the mixed herding and crop-raising skills developed in the previous millennia in the Near East. It must have been but one among many such small settlements on natural rises, safe from the annual flooding, that were able to exploit the natural food resources, rich soil, and riverine communications, provided by the Nile Delta. In contrast to Upper Egypt these people were buried within their settlements with virtually no grave equipment. In a slightly later settlement, about 5000 B.C., on the shores of Lake Moeris in the Faiyūm ("A"), the people lived in primitive huts, practising simple husbandry; growing emmer wheat and barley, which they stored in underground granaries; fishing and hunting game. Basketry and straw mats were skilfully woven; flax cultivated for linen making. Pottery was simple, often of coarse fabric, sometimes burnished but never incised or painted. No metal was used, but stone arrow-heads, axe, adze and sickle-blades were efficiently made. Long-distance foreign connections are reflected in the use of shells from the Mediterranean and Red Sea.

The first communities so far traced in the valley of Upper Egypt were identified at their cemeteries in the Badari District (*Badarian*) through excavations by Brunton in 1922-25, and in a small settlement site in the same region, at Hammamiya on a spur overlooking the valley, excavated by Miss Caton Thompson in 1924-25. The presence of simple copper awls and beads, and of glazed steatite beads, probably imitating turquoise, indicate a later stage of development than

6. Fragment of a large jar of black-topped ware, decorated in relief with the Red Crown, later associated with Lower (northern) Egypt; later Naqada I period (S.D. 35-39), *c.* 4300-4000 B.C., from Naqada, grave 1610.
(Ht. 8.9 cm; 1895.795).

that represented in the Faiyūm, though the economy was still based on simple subsistence farming and hunting. The manufacture of baskets, mats, leather garments and blankets, and the weaving of linen are all more accomplished than in the Faiyūm. Some Badarian pottery is exceptionally fine, made of a well-burnished, thin fabric, often with a distinctive ripple surface and black top, which may ultimately derive from pottery of Neolithic cultures now best known at Khartoum in the Sudan. Stone tools include bifacially retouched sickle-blades and hollow-based arrow-heads. Small figurines, animals on spoon-handles and a few amulets carved in bone or ivory are the only decorated objects. These people were the first to use the slate cosmetic palettes which were later so richly decorated. Burials of cows, jackals and sheep wrapped in shrouds in the same cemeteries as human beings may anticipate the place animals were to play in developed Egyptian religion.

At Hammamiya the Badarian culture was followed by the first stage of the predynastic period: *Amratian* (Naqada I), *c.* 4000-3500 B.C., which appears to have developed from it, though these people were to be the first to exploit the naturally irrigated valley. They have been traced, again largely through cemeteries, from Deir Tasa near Badari south to the First Cataract, notably at Naqada, Hu (Diospolis Parva), el-Mahasna and el-Amra. Copper is still scarce, but stone tools, particularly fine knife-blades, were skilfully made by first grinding down and then pressure-flaking the flint. A new type of red burnished pottery was decorated in white with geometric designs and less commonly with scenes of ritual dancing, hunting and weaving (*pl.* 4). Stone vases appear only rarely. Ivory combs have long teeth and backs ornamented with animals in silhouette slate palettes were also cut in animal, fish and human shapes. Baked clay female figurines were placed in graves. Rare vases bear the symbol later used to represent the fertility goddess. Evidence for buildings is scanty. An isolated fragment of a model fortified wall with two men on guard duty, found at Abadiya, is displayed in the Ashmolean.

About 3500 B.C. certain marked cultural changes in Egypt reveal the slow growth of an urban society with established political organization and traditions. This appears to have been largely a local development, though increasing trade with the Near East, bringing luxuries like lapis lazuli into Egypt, also encouraged cultural contacts which may have stimulated the emergence of mud-brick architecture and writing. Cemeteries, and rare settlements of this *Gerzean* culture (Naqada II) spread more widely then Amratian ones, extending in its fullest development from Lower Egypt as far south as Lower Nubia. No sites are yet known in the Delta, and virtually none between Badari and the Faiyūm. Increasing technical skill in working

7. Fragmentary limestone macehead of the Pharaoh 'Scorpion', shown wearing the White Crown of Upper (southern) Egypt; from the 'Main Deposit' in the temple precinct at Hierakonpolis, *c.* 3000 B.C. (Ht. 32.5 cm; E.3632).

metal, especially a greater use of silver and production of copper axes, daggers and knives, in pottery making, involving the use of the slow wheel and selected fine clays, in flint flaking and in the production of hard stone vessels, mark the rapid growth of specialist industries. The existence of substantial mud-brick architecture is best evidenced by a tomb-model of a house from el-Amra. Not only symbols, but perhaps also rites, associated with leading deities of dynastic times like Hathor, Neith, Min and Horus, used to decorate pottery, indicate the steady growth of organized religion. Scenes painted on pottery also show the reed-built, oar-propelled, boats used on the Nile (*pl. 5*) and sail-driven boats with high prow and stern,

long thought to be the sea-going vessels of foreigners, but probably also local river boats.

Since this period was to culminate in the First Dynasty, particular interest attaches to any archaeological evidence which will illuminate this fundamental and far-reaching political event. The accumulating signs of change in the material culture of Egypt in the last quarter of the fourth millennium B.C. are too various and their outcome too distinctively Egyptian for their origin to lie in foreign invasion. At this time, as imported cylinder seals and certain artistic and architectural motifs bear witness, Egypt definitely became closely acquainted with the urban civilizations in Elam and Mesopotamia at the head of the Gulf, either

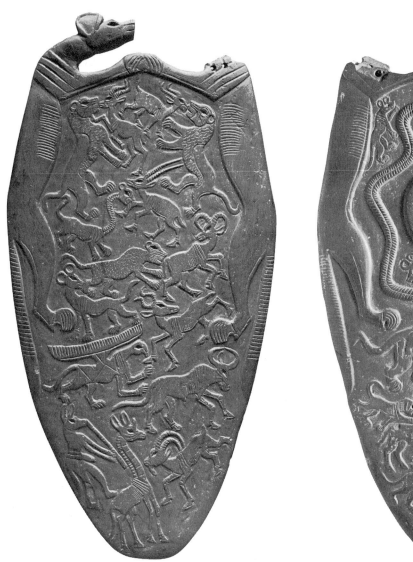

8. Ceremonial slate palette carved on both sides with animals, some in combat, some prancing to the music of a jackal-headed flautist. Two dog-like creatures flank the upper edges, and the necks of two mythical beasts snake around the reservoir for grinding eyepaint. From the 'Main Deposit' at Hierakonpolis, *c.* 3000 B.C. (Ht. 42.5 cm; E.3924).

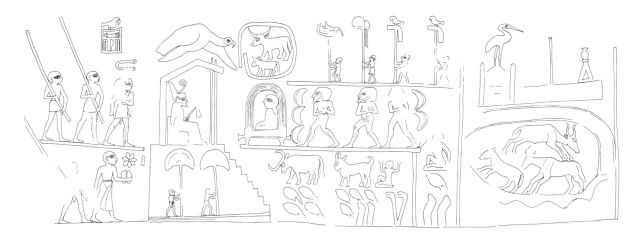

9. Drawing of the scenes carved in relief around the limestone macehead of Pharaoh Narmer: the king himself sits at the left, under a canopy, accompanied by fan-bearers and attended by his sandal-bearer and guards with staves, above whom the royal name — 'The Horus Narmer' — is written in a *serekh*, the frame emblematic of the palace. Beyond the captives and booty which he is apparently surveying is a shrine surmounted by an ibis-like bird, and an enclosure with cattle. The macehead was found in the 'Main Deposit' at Hierakonpolis and is dated *c.* 2900 B.C. (Ht. of actual macehead 19.8 cm; E.3631).

through sea-borne trade round the Arabian Peninsula or more probably by land routes through Syria and Palestine. But such cultural influences as this brought were soon modified to an Egyptian pattern. At Naqada, in cemetery T, and at Hierakonpolis, there are small cemeteries of Gerzean graves which closely anticipate in form and fittings the later royal tombs of the First Dynasty at Abydos. On the walls of the rectangular, brick-lined and plastered tomb 100 at Hierakonpolis, the very place traditionally associated with the rise of kingship, was painted a large frieze composed from a variety of scenes whose narrative unity is not obvious, though the role of chieftainship might be taken as a main theme. It is an isolated, but highly significant, sign that the creation of a bureaucratic state with written (i.e. pictorial) records was steadily advancing in Gerzean times, quite independent of foreign stimulus. The gradual development of decorated palettes as the earliest documents of royal activity, using a pictographic script quite unlike those of Sumer and Elam, and the representation of the crown later to bc associated with Lower Egypt on a black-topped potsherd emphasize the strength of this native tradition (*pl.* 6). Of political organization itself archaeology reveals little. It is still not clear whether the 'Union of the Two Lands' (i.e. Upper and Lower Egypt) was a real event or whether it is a projection backwards of the later pervasive dualism in Egyptian thought. There may well have been a more diverse, gradual centralization of various social units.

The Protodynastic Period (Dynasties I-II)

Two excavations, those of Quibell and Green at Hierakonpolis and Petrie at Abydos, both extremely well represented in the Ashmolean Collections,

allowed Petrie to unravel the architecture of the funerary monuments at Abydos, identify their royal owners and thereby establish the order of succession of the earliest pharaohs so accurately that subsequent work has merely modified his conclusions. The fragment of a large votive macehead found at Hierakonpolis, now in Oxford (*pl.* 7), shows a ruler known today as 'Scorpion', after the only surviving indication of his identity, wearing the White Crown. He may well be the pharaoh better known by the name Narmer, whose monumental slate palette from Hierakonpolis, now in Cairo, shows him wearing both the Red and the White Crowns on separate occasions. It is such monuments that have reinforced the view that Narmer was the key figure in the political unification of Egypt. A similar palette in the Ashmolean bears an elaborate design of animals whose symbolic significance, if any, is now lost (*pl.* 8). On a smaller, complete ceremonial macehead in Oxford, again from Hierakonpolis, Narmer is shown wearing the Red Crown, enthroned and protected by the vulture godess of Hierakonpolis. Before him are men bearing various nome standards, captives and numerals representing 120,000 men, 400,000 oxen and 1,422,000 goats captured in war, as well as a lady in a litter, who might be a captured princess (*pl.* 9). The legendary *Menes* of later sources, who begins Dynasty I, is probably to be identified with Narmer or his successor Aha.

At Abydos Petrie uncovered an unbroken series of tombs which were attributed on the evidence of inscribed mud sealings and stelae to the pharaohs Narmer, Djer, Wadji (Djet), Wedimu (Den), Queen Mer(it)Neith, Semerkhet, Ka (Qaa) (all Dynasty I) and Peribsen (Dynasty II); no stelae were found for Aha, Adjib (Anedjib) (Dynasty I) and Khasekhemwy

15

10. Basalt statue of a bearded man wearing a cap and a belt with penis sheath. Formerly in the collection of the Rev. William MacGregor, the statue is unique and its authenticity has been much disputed, though smaller male figures in ivory, attributed to the Protodynastic period (*c.* 2900-2650 B.C.), display some similarities: 'MacGregor Man' could be a forerunner of these, in the rarer medium of stone. (Ht. 39.5 cm; 1922.70).

(Dynasty II) though their tombs were also identified. Over 250 private stelae were found and numerous subsidiary graves were taken to be those of courtiers. A remarkably rich variety of objects from these graves, often very battered, and from the deposits at Hierakonpolis, notably carved ivories, sculptures and fragments of wooden objects, illustrate the great technical skill and artistic achievement of the craftsmen who served the first pharaohs (*pl.* 11). They also show that by the end of Dynasty II, represented in Oxford by the small statue of Khasekhem (*pl.* 12), the basis of Egyptian civilization was well and truly laid. Artistic conventions had been evolved which were to underlie all subsequent developments and hieroglyphic writing was rapidly becoming an instrument flexible enough for recording complex administrative procedures as well as religious and literary compositions.

Some doubt has been cast on the exact status of the 'royal' tombs at Abydos by Emery's subsequent discovery of another set of large tombs in a contemporary cemetery in the north at Saqqara. But neither the size nor the very scanty inscriptional evidence from Saqqara suggests royal occupants for these tombs. Indeed one of the rare inscribed stelae recovered from this cemetery may arguably be taken to identify one of the largest tombs as the grave of a nobleman who held a number of high offices late in Dynasty I.

Dynastic Egypt: Dynasties III-XXX

Old Kingdom: Dynasties III-VI (c. 2649-2150 B.C.)

Knowledge of this period depends much on the survival of sculptured reliefs and inscriptions in the tombs of royalty and nobility. From these the course of events, though rarely in detail, the character of the royal administration, the development of religious ideas and the nature of daily life at court and on the estates of great noblemen may be reconstructed, particularly in dynasties V and VI. As the great glory of the Old Kingdom lay in its architecture and monumental tomb-reliefs (*pl.* 2), no museum display can adequately document it. This must always be remembered, especially in Oxford, where the Old Kingdom collection is the weakest part of the historical display.

In 1901 at Beit Khallaf, just north of Abydos, Garstang excavated two immense brick *mastaba*-tombs (K.1, K.2) dated by sealings to the reigns of the pharaohs Sanakhte and Djoser, early in Dynasty III. They are represented in the Ashmolean by pottery and small objects. In Djoser's reign the court finally left Abydos and a new era is represented by the remarkable Step Pyramid, a developed *mastaba*-tomb, and its complex of temples at Saqqara designed for Djoser by his brilliant minister and architect Imhotep, whose legendary skill as a writer and healer was to lead later to his deification (*pl.* 13). The following rulers of the dynasty

I: Sandstone shrine erected by Pharaoh Taharqa (Dynasty XXV, 690-664 B.C.) in the court of the Temple of Amun built by him at Kawa in Nubia. The king is shown here on the north and west walls with the major gods of Memphis and Kawa. (3.95 × 3.95 × 2.57m; 1936.661).

are as little known as those of Dynasties I and II, though the step-pyramid of Djoser's successor at Saqqara, and the unfinished tomb of another king near el-Giza, show something of the dynasty's continuing prosperity. Monuments of Sanakhte and Sekhemkhet in Sinai suggest that they, as well as Djoser, campaigned successfully there, whilst Djoser at least had also asserted his authority in Nubia.

Their renowned pyramids virtually alone bear witness to the achievement of the rulers of Dynasty IV, for scarcely any record of historical events has survived. Though it is the more famous group of pyramids at el-Giza created by Khufu (Cheops), Khafrē (Chepren) and Menkaurē (Mycerinus) for which the dynasty is best remembered, the first pharaoh, Snofru, was alone associated with three pyramids, one at

Maidum, two at Dahshur. In the Ashmolean some fragments of relief sculptures from courtiers' tombs at Saqqara, Maidum and el-Giza, an important fowling scene from the tomb of the Lady Itet and her husband Nefermaat at Maidum, made by a unique process of filling cutout shapes with pigment, and a tiny fragment of painted fresco from the same tomb, reveal something of the way in which the tombs of the high officials who surrounded the king in death as in life, were decorated.

In the fourth and following dynasties the rulers of Egypt penetrated further into the surrounding countries: Libya, Nubia and Sinai, to protect their frontiers and ensure the ready supply of valuable raw materials and exotic luxuries through trade or conquest. At Byblos in the Lebanon, a vital source of timber, an

11. Lapis lazuli statuette of a woman; the head and body were made (and found) separately, and are held together by means of a peg; the eyes are hollowed out for inlays. From the temple enclosure at Hierakonpolis, *c*. 2900 B.C. (Ht. 8.9 cm; E.1057).

Egyptian temple was established as early as Dynasty IV. Records of temple building and the introduction of Sun Temples at Abusir and Abu Gurab reveal that the priesthood of Heliopolis and the cult of Rē was dominant in Dynasty V. Although royal pyramids were now planned on a smaller scale than before, their temples were decorated with the greatest skill. It is in the pyramid of Unas, last pharaoh of this dynasty, that the famous 'Pyramid Texts' first occur. This collection of spells was to help the pharaoh through the next world.

By Dynasty VI the great achievements of the Old Kingdom were past, though now tomb inscriptions of distinguished courtiers reveal more of the pharaoh's activities. This is in itself significant, for in this dynasty more and more power passed from the pharaoh into the hands of an increasingly influential provincial aristocracy. The enormous building operations of earlier rulers and lavish grants of funerary endowments to royal favourites had impoverished the central authority, which, after the long reign of Pepy II, disintegrated in political confusion.

The First Intermediate Period and the Middle Kingdom: Dynasties VII–XII: (c. 2150–1640 B.C.)

This collapse of the central administration, *c*. 2150 B.C., opened up a period of protracted strife between the local princes who had assumed control of the regions into which Egypt was divided (nomes); their rivalries are vividly revealed in tomb inscriptions. At the same time Egypt's neighbours took the opportunity to infiltrate into the country, especially into exposed regions like the delta. After many years of internal instability Egypt was re-united under a Theban ruler, Nebhepetre Mentuhotpe II of Dynasty XI (*c*. 2061–2010 B.C.). He inaugurated a period of consolidation and rehabilitation. The central government was stabilized, the frontiers re-established, and mines and trade-routes reopened. At Deir el-Bahari the pharaoh built himself a very original mortuary temple comprising a pyramid in the midst of a columned hall, set on a platform approached by ramps; tiny fragments from its reliefs may be seen in Oxford.

One type of object regularly found in ordinary graves particularly distinguishes the declining Old Kingdom and the First Intermediate for the archaeologist. Late in the predynastic period, under Asiatic influence, Egypt had adopted the cylinder seal and turned it to its own uses in the Old Kingdom. But from the Dynasties VI to X, initially again under foreign, perhaps Syrian, influence, cylinders were replaced by small stamp-seals, their backs cut as geometric shapes, loops or animals, birds, insects, plants and various hieroglyphic signs. Among these seals were some carved in the shape of the common dung beetle (scarabs); a form which rapidly superseded all others (*pl.* 16). This common insect had long

12. Seated limestone statue of Pharaoh Khasekhem with conquered foes incised around the base; one of a pair found in caches in the temple enclosure at Hierakonpolis, the earliest surviving Egyptian royal sculpture in stone. Dynasty II, *c.* 2700 B.C. (Ht. 62cm; E.517).

II: Fragment of wall-painting from a private house at El-Amarna showing two of the younger daughters of Pharaoh Akhenaten and Queen Nefertiti seated at their parents' feet; 1353-1335 B.C. (0.40 × 1.65 m, 1893.1-41(267)).

been popularly associated with the life-giving powers of the morning sun, endowing any object on which it appeared with potent amuletic power.

Dynasty XII (*c*. 1991-1783 B.C.) was a period of outstanding achievement, later regarded as an historic golden age. Important political changes and a series of forceful rulers, whose portrait statues are among the most remarkable surviving examples of Egyptian art, helped ensure the central government's authority. The capital was moved from Thebes to a site, south of Memphis, on the border of Upper and Lower Egypt and the rulers were buried in pyramids at Lisht, Lāhūn, Dahshūr and Hawara. Unfortunately the other architectural projects of this dynasty were largely obliterated by later building. Although the power of provincial administrators was gradually eliminated, sculptured reliefs and paintings in the tombs of wealthy local officials near nome capitals like Qaw, Meir, Deir el-Bahari and Beni Hasan, still offer vivid, intimate glimpses of daily life on rich men's estates.

The most important royal festival in Egypt was the *sed*, celebrating the union of Upper and Lower Egypt and renewing the crown's authority. Always held at Memphis, it normally took place after the king had ruled thirty years and thereafter at three-year intervals. This ceremony is the subject of a group of sculptured fragments in Oxford which were excavated by Petrie at Memphis, where they had been re-used in a later building. Their date thus depends entirely on the style of the reliefs, which suggested Dynasty XII to Petrie, though earlier and much later dates have been argued. Numerous stelae (memorial stones) simply decorated with offering scenes and votive inscriptions, including biographical information, and inscribed administrative scarabs, reveal details of the personnel and organization of government at all levels. An unusual stela in Oxford commemorates the sculptor Sirē. The front is conventional, but on the reverse is cut a sunken panel with a standing figure of Sirē in relief.

A lively demand for raw materials obtainable only outside the Nile valley, to supply the needs of highly accomplished craftsmen, stimulated a vigorous foreign policy. Control over Nubia, which gave access to the gold mines east of Wadi Halfa and the caravan trade to the south, was secured by a system of fortifications and trading posts. More permanent arrangements were made to exploit the mines of Sinai for turquoise and copper. The 'walls of the prince', built to protect the delta from infiltrating Asiatics, did not impede an extensive trade by land and sea with Palestine and Syria, particularly with Byblos and Ras Shamra (Ugarit), for timber, metals, wine and vegetable oils. Some of the larger towns in this area may have paid tribute to Egypt, but Egyptian military intervention was rare. Egypt also traded regularly with Crete, sending ivory, faience, ostrich shells and precious stones in exchange

20

III: Amulets, beads and pendants. *From top left to bottom right:* carnelian leg and hand and gold *Heh* (eternity)-sign, Old Kingdom; red jasper heart, Bes-figures of faience, seated child of carnelian and faience *wedjet*-eye, New Kingdom; silver *ankh*, Nubian 'C' Group; haematite headrest, obsidian scarab, double plume of glass, figures of Duamutef and Qebehsenuef and a *djed*-pillar, all of faience, Late Period.

(Hts. of largest and smallest: 66mm and 13mm; 1914.662, 1924.381, 1914.658, EA 508, 1925.415, 1921.1148, 1890.1131, EA 524A, 1912.192, EA 947, QL 640, 1983.148, EA 798).

for timber, textiles, wine and vegetable oils. These connections are reflected archaeologically by the appearance of distinctively Cretan pottery on Egyptian sites (*pl.* 14).

In the Middle Kingdom the language and literature of Egypt was more developed and stabilized. *Middle Egyptian* remained the standard well into the New Kingdom and, for some monumental purposes, until the Graeco-Roman period. Many fine stories, didactic treatises and mythological epics originally composed in this period were used for centuries as model compositions in the schools of ancient Egypt. One of the finest, the 'Story of Sinuhe' may be seen (in later scribal copy) in the Ashmolean. Long funerary inscriptions painted on the wooden coffins characteristic of the period offer a wealth of information on current religious ideas.

In no other period is the daily life of ancient Egypt so well documented as in the Middle Kingdom, largely owing to the many 'funerary models', generally of wood or clay, then believed appropriate for ensuring by magical means a rich man's comfort in the hereafter. Models of houses and gardens, of stables, granaries, kitchens, bakeries, butchers' shops and the like peopled with servants actively engaged in their routine tasks and of Nile boats fully equipped with sails, oars and crew vividly evoke the bustle of daily life on a nobleman's estate (*pls.* X, 25). Equally remarkable is the walled town beside the valley temple of Senwosret III at Lahun, excavated by Petrie in 1890. Built to a regular plan to house both the officials and the workmen engaged on pyramid building in Dynasty XII it revealed much of the living conditions of lesser members of society. The houses yielded ordinary objects of daily life in quantity, many of them made of wood, leather and fabric; in the words of the excavator 'just as they were last handled by their owners'.

The Second Intermediate Period: Dynasties XIII-XVII (c. 1640-1532 B.C.)

Although the general political situation for most of the time is not in doubt, parallel rather than consecutive dynasties make it uncertain exactly how long the interval between Dynasties XIII and XVIII lasted. At first, at Thebes and Memphis, Dynasty XIII largely carried on the traditions of the Middle Kingdom and there was not the conspicuous decline in artistic standards which marked the First Intermediate. Then as the authority of this government slowly disintegrated local rulers at Xois in the western delta established an independent line of kings (Dynasty XIV), whilst Asiatics, who had been slowly infiltrating into the eastern delta for some time, established a separate northern kingdom, during the early eighteenth century B.C., with its capital at Avaris in the delta, a site of uncertain location. These 'princes of foreign lands' (Hyksos) as

13. Bronze statuette of the deified Imhotep, vizier and architect of Pharaoh Djoser of Dynasty III; Saite Period. (Ht. 15.5 cm; Fortnum B.5).

they were known to the Egyptians, captured Memphis *c.* 1640 B.C. but were then content to rule as overlords in southern Egypt, which still had its own dynasty of native rulers at Thebes (Dynasty XVII) exercising authority from Abydos in the north to Nubia in the south.

Although later Egyptian records portrayed this period as a time of oppressive foreign rule, contemporary evidence suggests otherwise. The Hyksos rulers sponsored temple building, and works of art and literature in the tradition of their Egyptian predecessors. They brought Egypt into closer contact with Western Asia and introduced a number of improvements in military methods: notably light horse-drawn chariots and the composite bow. It is now clear, however, that they did not have a distinctive culture of their own. The widely distributed 'Tell el Yahudiyeh' ware and certain types of scarab, once termed 'Hyksos', reflect growing international trade rather than exclusively Hyksos political activity. Scientific analyses have now shown the 'Yahudiyeh ware' to be the product of several centres in Egypt and the Levant.

At first the Theban rulers of Dynasty XVII accepted Hyksos tutelage. The movement to expel the Hyksos appears very much as the personal action of one Kamose, whose brother and successor Ahmose, founder of Dynasty XVIII, captured Avaris, drove the Hyksos from the delta and pursued them into Palestine. In this struggle the Theban rulers employed troops (Medjay) from Nubia. A group of these are represented archaeologically by cemeteries, with graves cut as pan-shaped cavities in the sand ('Pangrave People'), extending from Serra in the south to Deir Rifa in the north; small settlements have been excavated at Qaw and el-Mustagidda. The grave goods are very distinctive. The bodies were often clad in leather garments with a variety of jewellery, notably bracelets made from strips of shell and mother-of-pearl. Small bowls of finely made red, black or black-topped ware, with or without incised decoration are typical. Axes, daggers, arrows, bows and archers' wrist guards, of Egyptian type, appear regularly in unplundered male graves. Close to the graves pottery and crudely painted animal skulls were packed in shallow pits. In later graves Egyptian pottery, scarabs and jewellery appear more often.

The Earlier XVIIIth Dynasty (c. 1550-1353 B.C.)

As in Dynasty XII, the prosperity and stability of the early XVIIIth Dynasty depended largely on a group of very able rulers, trained from youth to succeed to the army command. Their power and authority as pharaoh rested on an absolute control of all organs of state, including the priesthood. Despite the military character of the rulers and the importance of the army the administration rested with highly trained civil officials

14. Imported Cretan vase and Egyptian objects of faience, stone and bone from a Dynasty XII grave at Abydos. (E.3295, etc., from tomb 416).

promoted from all levels of society on merit. A highly centralized and carefully graded civil service was controlled by a vizier for the south and another for the north: a vice-regent administered Nubia. Egypt's religion, and to some extent her political and economic life, was dominated by the cult and priests of Amon-Rē, with a great temple at Karnak in Thebes, home of the dynasty (*pl.* 28). The stability of the system was demonstrated within a century of its creation during the minority of Thutmose III, when, contrary to all tradition, Queen Hatshepsut assumed full pharaonic powers.

Two important groups of objects from early New Kingdom foundation deposits, in the Ashmolean, illustrate an important aspect of the pharaoh's religious role. The earlier is from the magnificent, and in many ways very original, funerary temple at Deir el-Bahari in Thebes designed for Hatshepsut by her favourite Senmut. The later group is from a lesser temple at Koptos built by her successor Thutmose III early in his reign. The pharaoh ideally carried out in person the foundation ceremonies at all important new temples. These began with a survey of the site, including astronomical observations to fix the four corners, then the pharaoh himself made and laid four corner bricks. Sets of model tools, inscribed plaques and vessels, and other objects were deposited at intervals along the line of the walls, often allowing the archaeologist valuable indications of the original ground plan and a close date, through the royal inscriptions, for its foundation.

The policies of the earlier XVIIIth Dynasty kings were largely directed to avoiding another foreign domination. Egyptian influence was re-established in the south: the very important office of viceroy of Kush was instituted by Ahmose, and his immediate successors extended their authority beyond the Third Cataract, rebuilding the Middle Kingdom forts in that region (see also p. 58). In the west the Libyans were brought under control. But it was to the north-east, whence the Hyksos had come, that rulers like Thutmose I and III devoted their greatest energies, extending Egyptian authority well into Syria. This military and diplomatic involvement brought enormous prosperity to Egypt. Slaves, raw materials and manufactured goods came as war spoils, tribute or gifts; exploitation of mines in Nubia and the eastern desert yielded gold in quantity and trade brought exotic goods from lands like Punt. All was vividly portrayed in monumental temple reliefs or on the painted walls of courtiers' tombs. The furnishings even of lesser graves indicate in the foreign pottery they contain the flow of commerce into Egypt from Cyprus and the Levant.

Stimulated by the patronage of triumphant pharaohs and a rich court, national prosperity and foreign

IV: Statuette of the god Ptah, of bronze partly coloured black and inlaid with gold and silver, Late Period. (Ht. 17.8 cm; 1986.50).

 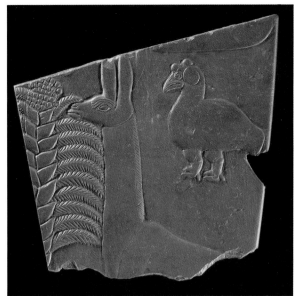

V: Front and back of a fragment from the centre of a slate palette (see *pl.* 8): captives with tribal standards; guinea-fowl, gazelle and palm tree; Abydos, Protodynastic period. (15.3 × 16.5cm.; 1892.1171). Photograph by Werner Forman.

contacts, all arts flourished, but still in the well-established traditions. Great Temples at Deir el-Bahari, Karnak and Luxor, royal tombs in the Valley of Kings at Thebes, even in their present battered state, bear witness to a period of unparalleled achievement in architecture and sculpture. The best work of this period in the arts is of unmatched technical skill and splendour, but there is much which suffers from an unrestrained love of colour and ornament. This is most strikingly seen in the minor arts and crafts which flourished as never before: coloured glass and faience vases and inlays; objects carved from wood, ivory or stone or made from baked clay in the form of animals, girls or dwarfs clearly designed to amuse; fine wood-work, leatherwork, metalwork and weaving. All are represented in the Ashmolean by groups of objects from graves at Abydos (*pls.* XIII, 23).

The Amarna Period and its Aftermath
(c. 1353-1307 B.C.)

In the earlier XVIIIth Dynasty the primary god in Egypt was Amon-Rē, who combined the person of Amūn, local god of the capital at Thebes, with the ancient sun-god Rē of the city of Heliopolis. This latter god had three main aspects, represented by the actual sun-disk (Rē: *Sun*), the falcon (Horus) and the falcon-headed man (Rē-Harakhty). During the reign of Amenhotpe III the role of the sun-god as a sun-disk (Aten) gradually gained in importance until in his successor's reign it provided the basis for a religious revolution unparalleled in Egyptian history. Under the

pharaoh's direct inspiration and close guidance a unique attempt was made to discard all the numerous gods of Egypt and their worship in favour of a single, universal god, the Aten. Inevitably by his remarkable independence of mind and action in religious matters Amenhotpe IV (Akhenaten) has attracted more attention than any other single figure in Egyptian history. Sadly, despite some spectacular archaeological discoveries, knowledge of his reign, its origins, course and aftermath remains extremely restricted and at many points highly controversial. The Ashmolean contains a very important and comprehensive collection from el-Amarna (Akhetaten), Akhenaten's new capital.

Akhenaten (1353-1335 B.C.) (*pl.* 18) was the son of Amenhotpe III and Queen Tiye. His father survived until at least his 38th regnal year and was buried at Thebes; whether or not he shared his throne at the end of his reign with his son and, if so, for how long is still uncertain. For a few years at the beginning of his reign Amenhotpe IV remained at Thebes, but in this time significant changes are apparent. Until this time the Aten had been shown in falcon-headed human form, like the elder god Rē-Harakhty, and bore a didactic name written without cartouches; after it the god was represented as a sun-disk with rays ending in human hands offering 'life-signs' to the pharaoh and his family, and his name was written, like a royal name, in cartouches. During these years there was also a radical change in the style of Egyptian art under the direct control of the Pharaoh (*col. pl.* II). The new pharaoh's single-minded allegiance to the Aten threw

25

15. Quartzite head of a young prince of the earlier part of Dynasty XVIII.
(Ht. 17cm; Queen's College Loan 1203).

him into increasingly sharp conflict with the priests of the established cult of Amon-Rē at Thebes. The royal name was changed from Amenhotpe: 'Amun is pleased' to Akhenaten: 'He who is serviceable to the Aten'. Then about his fifth regnal year a new residence for the Aten, the pharaoh and the court was established on a virgin site at el-Amarna, halfway between Thebes and Memphis, with the name Akhetaten: 'Horizon of the Aten'. Here the pharaoh, his queen Nefertiti (*pl.* 17) and their six daughters resided until his death, in or soon after his seventeenth regnal year. Between regnal years 9 and 12 the Aten had received a new name finally eliminating all traces of the old polytheism: 'Life to Rē, ruler of the two horizons, who rejoices in the horizon in his name Rē, the father who is come as Aten'.

Akhenaten's immediate successor was named Smenkhkarē. Nothing is known of him (if indeed it was a man and not Nefertiti by another name), nor of his parentage, nor how long, if at all, he survived Akhenaten. Then succeeded the best known, if politically one of the least significant, of all Egyptian phar-

aohs, Tutankhaten; so famous because his tomb was uniquely to be preserved more or less intact into modern times. Possibly the son of Akhenaten by a wife other than Nefertiti, he was married to one of Akhenaten's daughters and, since he was only about seven or eight at his accession, effective power lay in the hands of his eventual successor Ay, a high ranking military and civil official at Akhenaten's court. In the third or fourth year of his reign the court abandoned el-Amarna and returned to Thebes. The cult of Amun was restored and the cult of the Aten execrated; the pharaoh's name being changed to Tutankhamun. After a reign of about ten years he died and was buried by Ay in the famous tomb in the Valley of Kings at Thebes, found by Howard Carter in 1922. Ay briefly succeeded him and was buried in the same place.

Dynasties XIX-XXIV (c. 1307-712 B.C.)

The transition from dynasties XVIII to XIX is marked by Horemheb (1319-1307 B.C.), a man of unknown origin, who had attained high military and a civil rank by the reign of Tutankhamun. He dismantled

16. Limestone commemorative scarab of Amenhotpe III (*c.*1391-1353 B.C.) recording the number of lions shot by the king in the first ten years of his reign. (Ht. 8.3 cm; E.3895).

Akhenaten's temples at Thebes and built extensively himself. He had appointed his vizier Pramesse, whose family came from the Delta, to succeed him; as Ramesses I this person ruled only for about a year. His son Seti I (1305-1290 B.C.) maintained the traditions established by Horemheb as a major builder, who systematically removed traces of the Amarna pharaohs. It was the internal stability established by Horemheb that enabled him, and his successors, to campaign extensively in Western Asia against major powers like the Hittites with their local confederates in Syria, and to repulse, in the Delta, the first attacks of migrant peoples from western Turkey and the Aegean, the so-called "Peoples of the Sea" (amongst whom were to be found the Philistines). Mercenaries, drawn from these intruders, may be represented by a series of deposits found by Petrie at Ghurab. There, in shallow pits, cut beneath house-floors, a large quantity of personal property, including a certain amount of Mycenaean pottery and local imitations of it, had been burnt, smothered by sherds and covered by a relaid floor. No bones were included. This practice is unique in Egypt.

In a very long reign (*c.* 1290-1224 B.C.) Ramesses II perpetuated his fame in a series of enormous buildings decorated with reliefs of his military triumphs and gigantic statues of himself and his queen. Although he built temples in most of the major cities in Egypt, his most remarkable monuments are the rockcut temples of Abu Simbel, recently saved from encroaching Nile waters, and his funerary temple, the Ramesseum, at Thebes. This dynamic pharaoh is represented in Oxford on a stela from a temple he had built for the goddess Isis at Koptos. Set up by the overseer of works, Nebnakhtuef, it shows Ramesses II offering incense to the sacred boat of Isis carried by twelve priests (*pl.* 19). Thirty years after the death of Ramesses II dynastic intrigues and foreign pressures brought the dynasty to an end in political chaos.

Sethnakhte, who restored order and founded Dynasty XX ruled, like Ramesses I, for only a few years. His successor Ramesses III (*c.* 1194-1163 B.C.), the last great pharaoh of the New Kingdom, reorganized the internal administration, and the army, crushed a major rebellion in Libya and repulsed, in two great land and sea battles, the 'Peoples of the Sea',

VI: Painted wooden tomb model of a woman grinding corn from grave 604 at Sidmant; VIth Dynasty. (Ht. 18.8cm.; 1921.1423).

VII: Glazed faience shawabti and libation vessel, inscribed for the priest of Amun, Amenemope; from Theban tomb 148, XXth Dynasty, (Hts. 9.0cm, 10.7cm; Fortnum C.2, 1964.706).

who had already destroyed the Hittite Empire and were overrunning Syria and coastal Palestine. His achievement was immortalized in the sculptured reliefs of an enormous mortuary temple at Medinet Habu. Palace conspiracies and a strike of workers in the royal necropolis were the first signs of the political instability which during the next century forfeited for Egypt all influence in Western Asia, and all the wealth which that could give.

For more than a century after the end of Dynasty XX, *c.* 1070 B.C., northern Egypt was ruled by a dynasty with its seat at Tanis in the Delta, whilst from Thebes the High Priests of Amun, in hereditary sucession, assumed control over the south. By confining their spheres of influence the two authorities existed amicably side by side and princesses from Tanis married high priests in Thebes. A rapid decline in prosperity is reflected in the absence of major

17. Limestone column fragment showing Queen Nefertiti, accompanied by one of her daughters, making offerings to the Aten; from El-Amarna, *c.* 1353-1335 B.C. (Ht. 34cm; 1893.1-41 (71).

architectural undertakings and the independence of Syria and Palestine. Although Sheshonq I established a unified authority from his capital at Bubastis in the delta by breaking the succession of hereditary priests at Thebes the dynasty he established — XXII, *c.* 945-712 B.C.— was marked by constant unrest and divided authority. In the delta an independent dynasty — XXIII — was in control, *c.* 828-712 B.C., and the Theban High Priests remained very powerful. About 724 B.C. Egypt was invaded from the south by Piankhi, the native Nubian ruler at Napata (see p. 59).

Profiting from the country's divided state he rapidly advanced northwards and only at the Delta met serious resistance from the two rulers, Tefnakhte and Bocchoris, of the short-lived Dynasty XXIV (*c.* 724-712 B.C.).

Dynasties XXV-XXX (712-332 B.C.)

The Nubian rulers of Dynasty XXV (712-657 B.C.) brought stability and unity to Egypt for about a century, which in turn fostered a cultural and artistic revival marked by their special allegiance to the Theban god Amun and his cult. At Kawa in Nubia Taharqa, a later king of the dynasty, restored an old sanctuary of Amun, established in Dynasty XVIII, and built a new temple. A monumental shrine, decorated on the exterior with reliefs of the pharaoh paying homage to various deities (*col. pl. I*), and a kneeling stone ram with a figure of the pharaoh between its knees excavated from this building by Oxford Expedition to Nubia in 1930-1, are now displayed in the Ashmolean.

In the earlier seventh century B.C., the Assyrians, first under Esarhaddon, then under Ashurbanipal, provoked by Egyptian military assistance to their enemies in Palestine, invaded Egypt and established a political hegemony over a series of local rulers. Psammetichus of Sais (664-610 B.C.), son of one of these, with the help of Greek mercenaries, reunited Lower and Middle Egypt and established his authority over Thebes and the south as well. Preoccupied with troubles nearer home, the Assyrians left him to his own devices.

Dynasty XXVI, or the Saïte Dynasty (*c.* 657-525 B.C.), was the last great period of native rule in Egypt, distinguished by a growing involvement with the Mediterranean world as well as with Palestine and Syria, and a tendency in art and administration to revive the styles and practices of the Old and Middle Kingdoms. Egyptian intervention in Western Asia, after the end of the Assyrian Empire in 612 B.C., against the growing power of Babylon, notably under Nebuchadnezzar, was not always successful, but it briefly forestalled another invasion of Egypt. More immediately significant were the growing settlements

18. Painted sandstone statue of Akhenaten holding an offering table, head missing; from the garden shrine of a private house at El-Amarna c. 1353-1335 B.C. (Ht. 90 cm; 1924.162).

VIII: Copy in egg-tempera by Nina de Garis Davies of a detail showing a cat tied to a chair-leg from a wall painting in private tomb no. 130 (May) at Thebes; XVIIIth Dynasty. (1947.72).

of foreign merchants, primarily Greeks, established at various places in Lower Egypt. Outstanding among these was the community at Naucratis whose way of life is well illustrated by finds from excavations there under Petrie in 1884-5, Gardiner, Griffith and Hogarth in 1899 and 1903. In Egypt at large an archaizing tendency is clear not only in art. The Pyramid texts were carefully studied and used once more in private tombs, old administrative titles and offices were revived and royal authority was displayed in time-honoured forms. This relatively brief revival was abruptly ended when in 525 B.C. under Cambyses, the Persians, who had already overthrown the Babylonian Empire, invaded and captured the whole of Egypt. For the next two hundred years Egypt was intermittently a satrapy (province) of the Persian Empire.

For the first time Egypt became part of Western Asia. Persian rule may at times have been oppressive, but generally, despite later traditions, it was to the country's advantage. The Persian rulers brought new administrative efficiency, codified laws, undertook public works and sponsored temple building in the tradition of their pharaonic predecessors. In art and architecture Egyptian styles went virtually unchanged; Persian influence may only be detected in the Persian dress of certain official statues and in minor details. Though government business was conducted in Aramaic, the *lingua franca* of the Persian Empire, the native population still used their native language and the demotic script. It was at this time, about 450 B.C., that the famous Greek historian Herodotus visited Egypt and wrote the first full account of the country to have survived.

Egypt in the Graeco-Roman World

In 332 B.C. Egypt was released from Persian rule by the campaigns of Alexander the Great, who during a brief stay in Egypt carefully assumed the traditional role of pharaoh. After his death in 323 B.C. in Babylon, his body was brought to Egypt and eventually buried in the recently founded city of Alexandria. In the division of Alexander's Empire which followed his death Egypt fell to his general Ptolemy who, on the death of Alexander's Macedonian heirs, assumed full powers and extended his control over Palestine, Cyprus and Cyrenaica. For the next three hundred years the foreign ambitions and dynastic intrigues of the Ptolemies drew Egypt fully into the political and diplomatic life of the Mediterranean world. Hellenistic influence in Egypt was much greater and more pervasive than that of the Persians. Though traditional religious practices were respected and some of Egypt's greatest temples built at this time, both Greek and Asiatic gods were absorbed into the state pantheon. In administration, in military affairs and in art Greek ideas and methods took a firm hold. Although the Ptolemies are shown on monuments with all the outward signs of traditional pharaonic power, the royal names and titles written in cartouches, they developed the royal office in fresh ways (*pl. 20*). Commerce was directly stimulated and extensive patronage was extended to all aspects of learning.

In the first century B.C. increasing dynastic intrigues and the growing interest of Rome brought the dynasty to an end and Egypt formally became a Roman province in 30 B.C. on the suicide of Cleopatra and the execution of Caesarion, the son she had borne Julius Caesar.

Egypt under Rome and Byzantium, 30 B.C. to A.D. 641

Even without the rich legacy of documentary evidence the impact of Roman rule in Egypt would be clear

IX. Upper part of a steatite statuette of the military officer Huy and his wife Nay, 'Songstress of Amun'; Dynasty XVIII. (Ht. 14.7 cm; 1964.296).

33

19. Limestone stela dedicated to the goddess Isis by the overseer of works in the Temple of Ramesses II at Koptos, showing the king offering incense to the sacred boat of Isis carried by priests; from Koptos, Dynasty XIX. (Ht. 98 cm; 1894.106d).

20. Sculptor's trial-piece of limestone with details drawn in red, showing a profile head of Isis or a Ptolemaic queen as Isis; on the other side is the head of a king. (Ht. 10.3 cm; 1919.50, Beazley Gift).

from the archaeological record. Among everyday household equipment baked clay nozzle-lamps of Mediterranean type, blown-glass vessels, iron tools, metal locks and keys and lathe-turned woodwork reflect the change. The ox-driven waterwheel and the threshing-sledge supplemented older farming methods. Dress and jewellery shared the styles and fashions of the eastern Roman Empire. Terracotta figurines became the commonest type of votive offerings and household images (*pl*. X). Egyptian deities were assimilated to Hellenistic ones and the iconography of the two traditions was often inextricably and extravagantly blended. Deities like Bes, Harpocrates, Serapis and Isis were particularly popular; with them are found a whole host of more explicit invocations of virility and fertility. As all are mould-made, often rather crudely, they must have existed in quantity from the second to fourth centuries.

Yet still the traditional culture of dynastic Egypt persisted, slightly impaired perhaps but not yet fundamentally changed. Indeed it deeply influenced its new masters in Rome, where Egyptian cults and fashions had considerable vogue, as much as in the homeland. The Roman emperors are shown in sculptured reliefs with all the traditional trappings of their pharaonic predecessors. Official patronage was extended to the long established cult centres, particularly in Upper Egypt, where temple building continued in the scarcely modified, time-honoured styles. Alexandria, though less privileged than under the Ptolemies, remained a rich port and a major cultural centre. The vigour of local scholarship in the old traditions is shown by the wide variety of surviving copies of demotic literary works made at this time. Equally important for modern scholarship are the many surviving papyri of Greek literature originally produced by an important Greek minority in the population with special status under the Roman administration.

A radical change in burial customs in the fourth century A.D. provides the first clear indication that the ancient Egyptian tradition was moving into eclipse. The old painted wooden coffins, plaster masks and mummy portraits (*pl*. XI), were abandoned and the bodies placed, fully clothed, in earth-cut graves of varying depth without elaborate fittings or superstructure. The realm of Osiris was clearly giving way to the Kingdom of Christ. Christianity in a distinctive Hellenistic tradition was established in Alexandria by the late second century A.D. Conversion of the native population was initially slow, but by Diocletian's persecution in the late third century it was spreading with increasing rapidity. Indeed the years of the Coptic Church of Egypt are still numbered from A.D. 284, the date of Diocletian's accession.

In the Ashmolean, as in most museums, the term 'Coptic' (a corruption of the Greek word *Aigyptos*) is

X. Painted terracotta statuette of Roman date, showing the goddess Isis holding a tympanon; her crown is of traditional Egyptian form, but the figure in other respects illustrates the assimilation of Egyptian to Hellenistic deities. (Ht. 30.5 cms; 1889.1226).

XI: Mummy portrait of a young woman of the 4th century A.D.: from er-Rubayat, in the Faiyum.
(Ht. 38.0cm; 1966.1112).

21. Fragment of limestone relief, possibly depicting the story of Leda and the Swan; Coptic, fifth century A.D. (33 × 56.5 cm; 1970.403).

used generally to describe the art of the Egyptian Christians, particularly in the period up until the ninth century A.D. before increasing Islamic influence considerably modified its character. Even then the term is not always a happy one, since it is taken to embrace work of the fifth to ninth centuries A.D. which is Hellenistic rather than Christian in inspiration and often may not even come from Christian buildings. Crudely carved, yet lively sculptures, originally brightly painted, and textiles, which draw upon a repertory of motifs from classical ornament and mythology, are characteristic of the period (*pl.* 21). Christian subjects, haloed saints and biblical stories, only become common in the eighth century A.D.

In the later third and early fourth centuries A.D. the need for scriptures in the native tongue had stimulated the emergence of Coptic as a distinct literary language. After the Arab Conquest (A.D. 640) Coptic was gradually superseded by Arabic, becoming extinct as a spoken language in the sixteenth century. As the vocabulary of Coptic consists of ancient Egyptian words, supplemented by a considerable number of words borrowed from Greek, it was to play a vital role in Champollion's (see p. 5) decipherment of Egyptian

hieroglyphs, knowledge of which had disappeared soon after they were superseded in the Roman period.

Monasticism, both the rigorous dedication of the solitary hermit and the communal way with a set rule, was Egypt's most original contribution to the Christian heritage. Religious persecution, economic depression and the relative ease of desert life in Egypt all combined to stimulate the movement in the third century A.D. In the next two centuries monasteries were established throughout Egypt united in fierce loyalty to the patriarch of Alexandria, who consequently exercised considerable authority in the contemporary oecumenical councils summoned to discuss disputed points of doctrine. Indeed so acute became the friction with the Byzantine authorities that at the fourth Council of Chalcedon in A.D. 451 the Egyptian Church was condemned for heretical opinions. Two centuries later, in A.D. 640, Egypt fell to the Moslems and what slight vestiges there were of the ancient Egyptian tradition disappeared. The Liturgical language of the Coptic Church alone maintained a tenuous link, though it was well over a thousand years before this would again be recognized.

2. Aspects of Daily Life in Ancient Egypt

Although so much of the archaeological evidence for the development of Egyptian civilization comes from tombs and temples, it is evident that the Egyptians were not, as is often assumed, a people morbidly preoccupied with death and the hereafter. On the contrary a more careful inspection of the evidence reveals a great interest in life and a full appreciation of its joys. The apparent obsession with the after-life arose directly from a deep-seated desire to ensure that the comforts of an earthly existence should be secured in eternity. Rich and poor alike were provided in their graves with the best they had enjoyed on earth. These funerary offerings, sculptured tomb reliefs, and the much rarer domestic fittings excavated on urban sites,

throw considerable light on daily life. Varying as this naturally did with passing time and social status it is impossible in a brief sketch to do more than draw out from an enormous range of evidence those aspects best illustrated by archaeological material.

Arts and Crafts

For the ancient Egyptians there was no distinction between fine art and applied art, both were aspects of a single activity — handicraft — written with a sign depicting the borer used to hollow out stone vases. The approach was always a practical one in which aesthetic considerations or problems of artistic communication as we would understand them played no

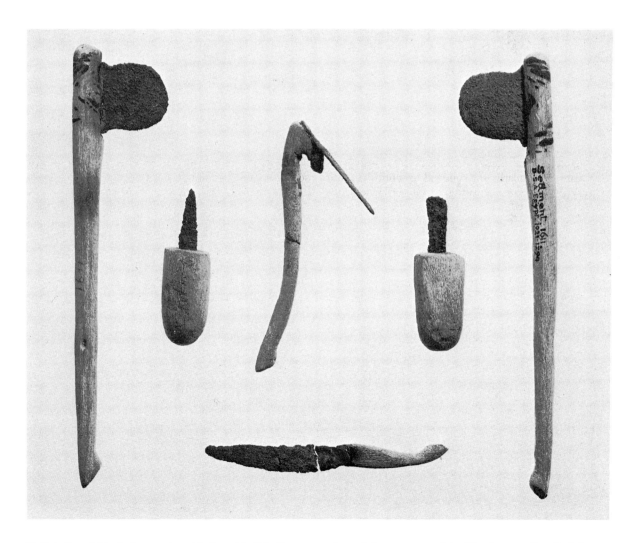

22. Set of model tools (axes, adze, chisels and knife) of copper and wood, from a grave of the First Intermediate Period at Sidmant. (Ht. of axes 11.6/11.8 cm; 1921.1294-1300).

part. Artistic personalities were virtually unknown. Sculptors or painters, like other craftsmen, were skilled and often highly trained artisans working in teams under an overseer. The images they created might incidentally be objects of beauty, but they were made primarily to secure by magical means the permanence of the personality or activity depicted. Inscription of the proper names and titles, not representation of distinguishing features, gave a statue its personal identity; switching or defacing these, not damaging or recutting the face and limbs, served to change it. Tomb reliefs of courtiers and officials enjoying their estates or engaged in religious ceremonies or on royal business were not records of particular occasions or things to be admired for the skill of composition and execution, but rather the best means to ensure material comfort and divine protection for ever. To this end the most durable materials and the most explicit representations were used.

With these points in mind it is easier to understand the essentially changeless character of Egyptian monumental art; its magico-religious inspiration inhibited radical change save, as in the 'Amarna Period', when a profound re-appraisal of religious ideas involved fresh concepts of the hereafter. Variations in detail there might be in response to foreign influence or changing social and economic conditions, but the underlying conventions remained fundamentally the same throughout dynastic times for all the major arts.

In preparing a two-dimensional scene for painting or *relief sculpture* preliminary guide lines and a squared grid were first drawn on the surface to ensure the resulting figures conformed to a standard canon of human proportions. It was this as much as anything which ensured the unity of style so distinctive of Egyptian art. Figures were almost invariably shown in profile with frontal eyes, shoulders were shown frontally, chest in three-quarter view and legs in profile. Hands and feet often show no distinction between left and right. Whether cut so as to leave flat projecting silhouettes or sunk into blocks the reliefs were always painted.

Little coherent pattern of sculptural development may be discerned in the variety of generally small-scale baked-clay models and stone figures made in Egypt during the predynastic period. Only towards the end of Dynasty II, notably in the Ashmolean statue of Pharaoh Khasekhem (*pl.* 12), is it possible to detect those unmistakably Egyptian characteristics which were subsequently to distinguish all *sculpture in the round*. These arise directly from the methods universally employed to carve stone statuary. Even with the

XII. Wooden model of a boat carrying soldiers, some playing a board game; from a rock tomb of the Middle Kingdom at Beni Hasan. (Length 71.5 cm; E.2301).

XIII: Pottery vessels in the shape of a calf, a seated girl and a hedgehog, from graves of Dynasty XVIII date at Abydos. (*Left to right:* ht. 10.2cm, E.2670 from D.29; ht. 13.9cm, E.2432 from W.1; ht. 7.4cm, E.2775 from D.11).

more flexible materials like wood, metal and faience the conventions were too powerful to escape. Stone statues were cut from roughly cuboid blocks approximating as closely as possible to the required dimensions. Preliminary guide lines and a squared grid comparable to that used for relief sculpture were first drawn on two sides. The unwanted stone was then chipped or ground away with copper or bronze tools and an abrasive. Features were normally conventional and even stones worked to a high polish were painted in natural colours. The figures which emerged, carved from front and side following the guiding grid, always retained something of the rigidity and cuboid form of the parent block. The widely used back pillars of Egyptian statuary served to emphasize this rectilinear form, though it is not known whether they were retained for symbolic or technical reasons. In looking at Egyptian statuary in a museum display it has always to be remembered that they were designed to be seen from the front, more rarely from the side, in an appropriate architectural setting in a temple or tomb.

Painting on plaster or wood allows for greater freedom of expression than carving and even the Egyptians, though adhering to conventions in representational painting, produced purely ornamental paintings on ceilings, walls and woodwork delightful in their vivacious colour and design. Such work was never fresco, but a form of distemper using water, alone or mixed with glue, as a vehicle for applying mineral pigments which provided a primary palette of red (iron oxide or ochre), yellow (ochre or orpiment), blue (powdered azurite or blue frit), green (malachite, chrysocolla or green frit), black (carbon) and white (gypsum or whiting).

If in the monumental arts the Egyptian genius often appears unimaginative and inflexible, even a rapid glance at the minor arts and crafts will reveal not only, as might be expected, a consummate mastery of materials, but also a much more adventurous spirit. As their sculpture reveals, no ancient people were more skilled in the manipulation of stone, often the hardest and most exacting available. In pre- and proto-dynastic times the great natural mineral wealth of Egypt was exploited with remarkable skill to produce a wide range of stone vessels, richly contrasted in form and colour, as food receptacles in tombs. From the Old Kingdom onwards shapes were more restricted, vessels smaller, stones softer, until production was largely confined to cosmetic vessels. In a land where gold, electrum and a range of semi-precious stones were readily available the jeweller's art naturally flourished, though here, particularly in the New Kingdom, technical skill and enthusiasm sometimes parted company with good taste in a riot of ornament. Since wood was relatively scarce and often of poor quality the *Egyptian carpenter* needed much native ingenuity (*pl. 22*). The results at their best bear comparison with the furniture of any age or place; well made with fine veneer, inlay

23. Glass vessels of Dynasty XVIII: kohl-tube in the form of a papyrus column, from Medinet Ghurab; small yellow vase, and dark-blue vase with white, yellow and blue stripes. (Hts. 8.9 cm, 3.5 cm, 6.8 cm; E.2578, 1959.438,1965.294).

and marquetry decoration. The carpenters' technical skill was best shown in chariot and boat building (*pl.* XII), their sculptoral enterprise in the decoration of toilet accessories, walking sticks, musical instruments and small-scale statuary. The lack of decorative enterprise shown by the Egyptian *potter* contrasts markedly in almost every period with that of his fellow craftsmen. After the predynastic period decoration is rare; but during the New Kingdom painted designs were again briefly in fashion and very attractive small cosmetic vases were made in human and animal shapes (*pl.* XIII).

Technical skill and love of colour found full expression in the manufacture of objects in *faience* and *glass*: two closely related artificial substances widely exploited by Egyptian craftsmen. Egyptian faience (not to be confused with the much later decorated earthenware named after Faenza in Italy) consists of a body material or core of sintered quartz covered by a vitreous, alkaline glaze, varying in colour. It was widely used after its first appearance in the predynastic period for beads, amulets and inlays, vessels and tiles, scarabs and statuettes, particularly shawabtis. As the chemical composition of ancient Egyptian glass is

essentially that of ancient glaze their discovery was no doubt very closely connected in the predynastic period, though glass does not seem to have been made intentionally, at least on anything but the smallest scale, until the New Kingdom when it was used for beads, inlay, vessels and statuettes (*pl.* 23). In the Late Period production declined very considerably, only to be revived in the Ptolemaic and Roman periods.

The extraction, smelting and casting of copper was practised in Egypt by the predynastic period, but bronze, an alloy of copper and tin (which occurs rarely in Egypt), was not introduced until the Middle Kingdom. It then became increasingly common until replaced by iron, which was a rare luxury until Dynasty XXVI and not commonly used for tools and weapons until Ptolemaic and Roman times. Though gold was readily available, silver was considerably rarer and only became less valuable than gold after the Middle Kingdom through increasing imports from Western Asia. Throughout the dynastic period the *metal-smiths* produced a very wide range of tools and weapons, though shaft-holes were only slowly adopted, toilet articles and sheet-metal vessels. Metal was only rarely used for statuary before the Late Period, but thereafter a variety of bronze statuettes of gods, sacred animals and emblems were regularly produced (*pls.* 28-32 and *col. pl.* IV).

Although a museum display cannot hope to reflect a civilization's architectural achievement, through fragments and models it may offer indications of styles and *building methods*. Sun-dried mudbricks were, as they still are, the characteristic building material of Egypt for all but the most monumental structures. Mud-plastered reeds provided primitive or temporary structures. In the dynastic period wood was used with the restraint its value imposed, generally for doors, sometimes for roofs, also occasionally for columns and architraves in temples. It was more common earlier as may be seen from the way in which early reed and wood methods of construction and decoration profoundly and persistently influenced Egyptian architectural style. With their deep-seated desire for permanence it was inevitable that once the Egyptians had achieved mastery of large-scale stone working they would exploit the rich local deposits of limestone, sandstone and granite to build the superstructures of funerary monuments and the most important temples. Domestic buildings of all sizes were built round open courtyards with little or no elaboration of architectural detail save among the richest classes. Similar principles were observed in temples where, set along an axis, an entrance pylon led first into the open, perhaps colonnaded, court, leading into a hypostyle or pillared hall (with small rooms adjacent for storage and services) which culminated in a dark sanctuary for the deity statue. Domestic buildings for the temple staff, workshops and stores clustered around the main building. Egyptian temples, like Medieval cathedrals, grew by accretion and restoration until what little unitary planning there might have been in the original structure was wholly obscured.

Writing and Literature

The ancient Egyptian language is related to Semitic tongues like Hebrew and Arabic, to certain East African languages, and to the Berber idioms of North

Figure 2. Range of languages and scripts used in Egypt from the beginning of the Dynastic Period to the Byzantine. (Reproduced from 'Literacy and Ancient Egyptian Society', *Man* 18, 572-99, by courtesy of the author, John Baines).

	3000	2500	2000	1500	1000	500	AD	500
Form of script	Early dynastic	Old Kingdom	First interm.	Second interm. Middle Kingd. New Kingd.	Third interm.	Late Period Graeco-Roman		Byzantine
Stages of Egyptian language	Invention of script	Old Egyptian	Middle Egyptian		Late Egyptian	Demotic		Coptic
Hieroglyphic	———————————————————————————————— 394[1]							
Cursive (from OK = hieratic)[2]	——————————————————————————————							
Cursive hieroglyphs			? ——————————					
Abnormal hieratic (Theban area)					———			
Demotic					————————— 452[1]			
Egyptian in Greek letters[3] (later Coptic)						... ———		
Greek[4]						..... ———		
Carian[5]						———		
Aramaic[6]						———		

[1] Latest dated inscription
[2] The earliest cursive forms are distinct from the monumental, but may not constitute a separate script 'hieratic'. Cursive is placed earlier because writing was probably invented for administration
[3] Used in magical texts
[4] Earliest dated inscription 591 B.C., official language from 332
[5] Language of mercenaries from Anatolia
[6] Administrative language of the Persian empire

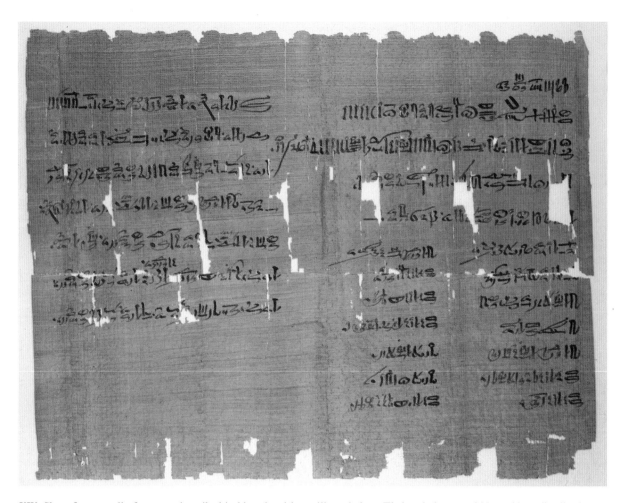

XIV. Sheet from a roll of papyrus inscribed in hieratic with a will made by a Theban lady named Naunakhte, distributing her property among the children of her two marriages: the document begins on this sheet, top right, with the date—year 3 in the reign of Ramesses V (*c.* 1156-1151 B.C.). (43.2 × 55.7 cm; 1945.97).

Africa. In its very latest form it is known as Coptic, because it was used by the Copts, the Christian inhabitants of Egypt. It was written in the Greek alphabet supplemented by seven special characters derived ultimately from the hieroglyphs of the earlier language. Most vital from the Egyptologists' point of view has been the survival of many ancient Egyptian words in the Coptic language, spoken by the Christian population of Egypt until the sixteenth century A.D. and surviving still as the ritual language of the Coptic Church. Arabic is the language of modern Egypt.

Three main scripts were used in dynastic and Roman times to write Egyptian (*fig.* 2):

1. *Hieroglyphic* (Greek: 'sacred carved' letters) was a conventionalized picture-symbol script used from earliest historic times, though its origin before *c.* 3000 B.C. is still obscure, until the fourth century A.D. At first all-purpose it gradually became the display or monumental script reflected in the name the Greeks gave it. Although initially the hieroglyphs were pictures of objects, animate and inanimate, directly expressing simple concepts in pictorial terms, they were rapidly employed in the syllabic spelling of words capable of expressing the many subleties of speech and thought. A determinative was placed after the syllabic spelling of a word to indicate the proper reading of the signs and to avoid ambiguity. The signs could be arranged vertically or horizontally, usually read from right to left, though by no means invariably. The direction is indicated by the animals, birds etc. which always face the beginning of the inscription. No divisions were made between words.

2. *Hieratic* (Greek: 'priestly' letters) a cursive modification of hieroglyphic is found sporadically in stone inscriptions from as early as Dynasty I, but

seems only to emerge in common usage from the later Old Kingdom; thereafter it was the chief documentary script (*pl.* XIV). It could be written either in vertical columns or horizontal lines, but the direction was exclusively from right to left. In the late New Kingdom an even more cursive script, known as abnormal hieratic, developed out of business hieratic only to be rapidly superseded by a third script.

3. *Demotic* (Greek: 'popular' letters) was a still freer script which remained in use from Dynasty XXVI to the fifth century A.D. as the main script in everyday use. It was always written in horizontal lines and read from right to left.

In pharaonic Egypt *papyrus* was the universal writing material except for ephemeral documents, notably school exercises, for which gesso-covered wooden writing-tablets or fragments of bone, stone and pottery (*ostraca*) might be used (*pl.* XV). The yellowish-brown colour and brittle state of surviving papyrus are the products of time and desiccation. When fresh, papyrus is generally whitish-yellow in colour and as flexible as modern paper. It was made from the soft inner cellular pith of freshly-cut green papyrus (*Cyperus papyrus*) stems. After the coarse outer rind had been removed the inner pith was cut into broad strips, which were then carefully placed side by side on a board in two layers, the second arranged crosswise over the first. The two layers were beaten with a mallet into a thin even sheet and left, probably in a press, to dry. The

XV. Limestone ostracon with a humorous sketch: a boy drives an animal, probably a baboon trained to pick fruit, while two chattering crows (rivals for the fruit?) look on; Dynasty XIX.
(12 × 10 cm; 1938.914).

24. Limestone statuette of a scribe and priest of Thoth, who served in the god's temple at Hermopolis in Dynasty XIX; he carries a baboon, Thoth's sacred animal. (Ht.31 cm; 1961.536).

red ochre respectively, powdered and mixed with a weak solution of gum and water. In dynastic times the pens were made from a rush (*Juncus maritimus*) which still grows in Egypt. The end was cut at an angle and lightly chewed to split the fibres and form a fine brush. Normally at least two pens were carried for black and red ink, but it was possible to use opposite ends of the same pen.

It is through the exercise done by student scribes that much of Egypt's literary heritage has come down to us. The training was long and thorough, but once fully equipped the scribe attained a position in society which carried with it considerable privilege and status.

In their language and literature, as in so much else, the Egyptians achieved a broad consistency and continuity over a very long period. The language developed in the Old Kingdom was still in official use over two and a half millennia later. In the form perfected in the Middle Kingdom (Middle Egyptian) it remained the standard for most monumental purposes until the Graeco-Roman period. Literary modes varied slightly from period to period and criteria of palaeography, vocabulary and syntax allow for distinctions in the dating of texts, but only in the 'Amarna Period' was the contemporary spoken idiom introduced into writing and the earlier literary language for the moment entirely discarded. Apart from their secular literature, the Egyptians have left a considerable legacy of religious works, letters, magical and scientific texts, not to mention business and legal records in great variety.

Food, Farming and Horticulture

As has already been described (*p.* 5) the fertility of Egypt depended upon the thin layer of rich earth deposited by the annual flood of the river Nile. The principal corn crops were barley and emmer until the Ptolemaic period when wheat became Egypt's main export (*pl.* 25). Oil was produced in large quantities for food, ointments and medicines, for cosmetics and for lamp fuel, with the *Moringa*-tree, castor-oil plant, sesame and saffron as the main sources. Flax, harvested in the winter, was the basis of the linen industry and another source of oil. Among vegetables, onions and leeks were particularly cultivated by the peasants as food; lettuces and radishes, gourds and melons, beans and lentils were also staple crops. In an almost treeless land cultivated trees were greatly valued, among them dom-palms and sycamore-fig, persea trees (*Mimusops schimperi*) and 'sweet-fruit' trees (*Balanites aegyptiaca*), pomegranates, acacia, tamarisks, figs and vines. Olive trees were never successfully cultivated. Wine was produced from grapes and dates. Honey was the main sweetening agent.

Animals were bred not only for food but also to supply the constant demand for temple sacrifices.

result was a pure white, perfectly pliable writing surface which had only to be trimmed with a knife and burnished with a pebble for use.

The very distinctive long, narrow palettes of the Egyptian scribe have cavities at one end for holding solid cakes of ink and a depression down the centre for pens varying from six to sixteen inches in length. Black and red inks were most commonly used, of carbon and

25. Wooden model granary with a scribe recording the contents (upper right), from a tomb of the Middle Kingdom at Beni Hasan. (Length 26.5 cm; E2311).

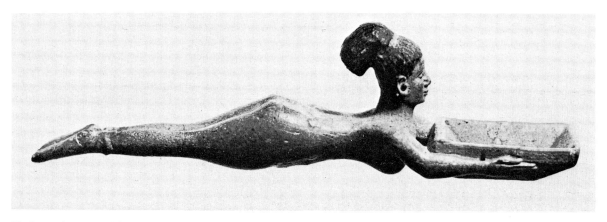

26. Cosmetic spoon of faience, in the shape of a swimming girl; from a tomb at Sanam in Nubia, Dynasty XXV. (Length 11 cm; 1921.735, from tomb 963).

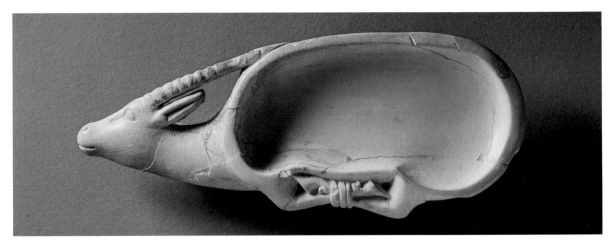

XVI. Cosmetic dish in the form of an ibex with bound legs, ivory; from a tomb at Qau, Dynasty XIX. (Length 15.4 cm; 1923.622, from tomb 562).

Oxen, sheep, goats, pigs and donkeys were the principal domestic animals; wild animals, like the antelope and oryx, were captured and fattened. Egypt was a land rich in water fowl: ibises, pelicans, cranes, cormorants, herons of all kinds, flamingoes, ducks and geese were netted and penned in winter for fattening. Although fish, like pork, were believed to be adhorrent to the gods, they were caught and eaten dried by the peasants.

Even a cursory glance at their sculpture and painting reveals the Egyptians' love of flowers and decorative plants. Egyptian ornament was dominated by the lotus and papyrus. The papyrus marshes, and the open country which lay behind the heavily cultivated banks of the Nile, provided the relaxation of hunting and fishing as well as the flowers so exotically combined as garlands and clusters for festivals and feasts. Private gardens were as much a source of pride as they were of sustenance; great care was taken in laying out gardens for temples, tombs and private houses. In Egyptian literature trees, flowers, music and love are inseparable, recurrent themes.

Costume and Cosmetics

Egyptian garments were of linen, draped and pleated, not tailored, and usually plain. Though fashions both in dress and hair-styles naturally varied, the main trends changed little. Men wore a loin cloth, a skirt or kilt, or an undershirt beneath a long flowing garment reaching from neck to feet. Women normally wore a loosely fitting dress reaching from shoulder level to below the knees. Both men and women of the upper classes wore wigs, sometimes very heavy and elaborate ones; women normally wore them over their own hair, men on a shaven head. Sandals were made of papyrus and palm-fibre, woven or plaited, and sometimes of goat or gazelles skin tanned and stained. The royal family wore elaborate head-dresses; courtiers a simple decorated circlet. Officials carried staffs of office and on ceremonial occasions wore jewellery — rings, anklets, bracelets, necklaces, ear-studs and ear-rings — made from a great variety of metals, minerals and faience.

Cosmetics were widely used and various toilet articles were deposited in graves from earliest times. The scorching winds and heat of Egypt made the use of unguents and pomades a necessity for the skin and hair. Scents and scented woods and herbs, pounded and mixed with oil, were rubbed into the body. Concern for personal hygiene and appearance is found in prescriptions in medical papyri for making hair grow or to prevent it turning grey, for removing unwanted hair, wrinkles and spots, for improving the skin and removing unpleasant smells. The range of toilet articles was constant, though great ingenuity was exercised at certain periods in varying their forms and the materials from which they were made. Toilet-boxes usually contained mirrors, combs, tweezers, pumice-stones and toilet spoons, with pots or boxes for the various cosmetics (*pl.* 26).

The two commonest eye-paints, both products of Egypt, were malachite (green ore of copper) and galena (dark grey ore of lead). Malachite is known from the predynastic period, but was generally superseded in historic times by galena. These substances are found in graves either in a raw state, packed in bags of linen or leather, or prepared for use as a paste or powder (kohl) in pots, vases and tubes. Lips were painted with a preparation of red ochre mixed in oil or fat; unmixed it was used as rouge. A mixture of oils and lime served as a cleansing cream. Henna was used to colour the soles of the feet, the palms of the hands, the nail and the hair. Tattooing was also long popular with men and women.

3. Religion and Funerary Customs

Religion and religious practices permeated the life of ancient Egypt in a way no western, certainly no modern western, man may easily appreciate. Even after the development of a complex bureaucratic state in the New Kingdom there was no real distinction between religious and secular. Despite increasing specialization all state officials remained, if no longer priests in fact, then servants of a head of state who was a god. Art and literature as well as life were deeply rooted in religion. Any phenomenon or outstanding event was traced back not to natural or historical causes but to the agency of the gods who were manifold. It was possible to deify a human being, to see divinity as much in plants, ani-

mals and forces of nature as in such qualities as 'truth' and 'fate'. More perplexing to a modern observer is the apparent ease with which any concept might be incorporated into the great body of theology without regard for its relation with existing explanations and ideas. What might appear self-contradictory to the modern view simply demonstrated to an ancient Egyptian the range and infinite potential of divine authority. In covering this extremely complex subject here particular attention has been paid to those aspects most commonly encountered in a museum display.

The remarkably varied character and often incongruously various forms of the Egyptian gods have long

27. Limestone stela showing a man and his wife adoring two cats described in the inscription as manifestations of the sun-god in two different aspects, Re and Atum; from Deir el-Medineh, Dynasty XIX. (Ht. 21.2 cm; 1961.232).

28. Bronze statuette of the god Amun-Re of Thebes; Late Period.
(Ht. 25.3 cm; 1933.1430).

been a source of fascination. The political unification which marked the opening of the dynastic period *c.* 3000 B.C., involved the fusion of many originally independent tribal cults. Each settlement in prehistoric times had its own deity, manifest in a material fetish or more commonly in some animal form (*pl.* 27). Although, as the developing religious cults of dynastic times gained coherence, these animal deities assumed human limbs and human characters, local patriotism and an innate conservation sustained individual differences. Thus it was that Thoth for instance, the scribe of gods and inventor of writing, may appear entirely in human form, in human form with an ibis or baboon head, or as an ibis or baboon (*pl.* 24). More confusion followed from a tendency to identify the local town-god with other gods who shared common characteristics or attributes. Many deities, for example, were assimilated with the prestigious sun-god Rē, whilst ever-increasing political pressures from the central authority stimulated the growth of an official pantheon and one supreme god, which varied with changing political circumstances. Two gods associated with capitals of the Old Kingdom, Ptah of Memphis and Rē of Heliopolis, retained their importance through dynastic times.

The ram-headed Arsaphes of Heracleopolis (Herishef) was briefly in the ascendent in the First Intermediate period, Neith, goddess of Sais, under Dynasty XXVI (Saïte). Amun who emerged as a supreme deity in the Middle Kingdom had an assured supremacy in the New Kingdom as the principal god of the Theban rulers who expelled the Hyksos (*pl.* 28). But only once, under the heretic pharaoh Akhenaten, was any attempt made at monotheism. Its unpopularity and rapid collapse on his death only serves to emphasize the multiplicity of the ever-hospitable Egyptian pantheon.

With such a range of deities and local traditions the mythology of Egypt was inevitably tortuous and complicated. The basic creation myth had three main forms; that of Heliopolis, the most widely adopted, may be briefly cited here. Atum ('The All') (*pl.* 29) emerged on a mound of earth in the waters of chaos and created Shu, god of air and Tefnut, goddess of moisture, in turn producing Geb, the earth-god and Nut the sky-goddess, parents of the pairs Osiris and Isis, Seth and Nephthys. The two former came to embody the forces of life and regeneration, Seth the destructive force. These nine deities ('ennead') were treated as a group of supreme gods at Heliopolis and in Egypt generally. An equally pervasive and important myth, again varying in details, centred on Osiris. Osiris, who had been an earthly ruler, was stealthily killed by Seth who then usurped his throne. Isis recovered her dead brother-husband's body and partially revived it. She retreated into hiding in the marshes and gave birth to Horus (*pl.* 30), who eventually avenged his father's death against Seth, later the god of storm, of deserts and foreign lands. In life each pharaoh was identified with Horus and in death with Osiris, the ruler revived to rule over the dead. The whole ritual character of Egyptian religion turned on this crucial god-king relationship which was intensely personal. Temple services were designed to enhance and perpetuate it. The priesthood were acting by proxy for the pharaoh, rarely able to officiate in person. Their interest (and remotely that of all Egyptians) was in ensuring that the services were rightly performed and this key relationship between god and pharaoh thereby preserved.

In this way Egyptian religion came to have two very distinct aspects, the one more fully understood today than the other. The state or official religion was an exclusive cult, the preserve of the priests in temple communities which served the gods in private. It was only through occasional public festivals that the people were drawn into temple worship and then only as spectators in special performances. The devious theologies and complicated mythologies which have survived from this side of Egyptian religion can have meant little to the illiterate population at large, whose religious beliefs must be gleaned from a variety of inarticulate archaeological evidence. Popular cults certainly grew up at the great shrines, but in the New Kingdom it is interesting that the most popular deities are foreign ones like Anat and Astarte. Of native gods great attention was naturally paid not to the powerful state gods, but to those who might be expected to lessen the dangers and burdens of daily life. Among these the grotesque dwarf Bes (*pl.* 31), who appears on a whole range of household objects, held a special place. Popular superstitions and magical practices are evident from the amuletic ivory wands of the Middle Kingdom and the later Cippi of Horus, designed to protect the owner from all nastiness (*pl.* 33).

In their *funerary practices and beliefs*, as in all aspects of their religion, the Egyptians were constantly assimilating fresh ideas without rejecting earlier ones not in harmony with them. Yet through all this complex range of customs ran a constant belief common to all ranks of society throughout dynastic times. Every Egyptian aspired to enjoy for eternity the best his rank on earth had led him to expect. To this end it was vital that his body should remain intact, supplied with the necessary food and drink, and his name endure. Naturally the wealthier a man was the more elaborate his provisions for the hereafter. Though the theological ideas implicit in these beliefs may not easily be summarized, and were moreover constantly changing, two concepts are regularly encountered. What is now referred to as the 'soul' was for the Egyptian his *Ba*, commonly represented as a human-headed bird,

29. Bronze statuette of the god Atum; Saite Period. (Ht. 23.5 cm; 1969.490).

30. Votive bronze statuette of Isis suckling the child Horus, excavated at Saqqara together with the original wooden throne and base; on the further side of the base is an ink incription in hieratic, and a second inscription in hieroglyphs on the bronze plinth asks 'May Isis give life to Hepiu'; Late Period. (Ht. 24.1 cm; 1971.101, gift of the Egypt Exploration Society).

31. Bronze statuette of the god Bes, protector of the household and pregnant women, holding a bowl; Late Period. (Ht. 4.7 cm; Fortnum B35).

32. Bronze statuette of an Oxyrhynchus fish with a worshipper: the base is patterned with the sign denoting 'water' in hieroglyphic script and inlaid with red and blue glass; Late Period. (Length 14.5 cm; 1983.236).

which left the body at death and thereafter enjoyed a life of its own. There is no close modern equivalent to the more important *ka*, for which all the funerary equipment and the tomb ('home of the *ka*') were made. Regarded as distinct from a person it embodied his 'personality' or 'temperament', even his 'fortune' and 'position'.

It was not until the New Kingdom that the processes needed to ensure adequate preservation of the human body were properly understood and even thereafter there seems to have been a variety of methods and much experiment. Basically it was a question of removing the brain and viscera and then preserving the body by treatment with natron (a form of salt), oils, unguents and resins before wrapping it in linen bandages and placing it in a coffin. In order to provide the mummy with magical protection a whole series of amulets (*col. pl.* III) might be placed in appropriate positions within the bandaging. Among an enormous variety of coffins attention may be called particularly to those of the Middle Kingdom. They were decorated with excerpts from a body of funerary texts, adapted from the royal 'Pyramid Texts' of the

later Old Kingdom (see p. 18), and with the two eyes of Horus, doors and palace facades, to ensure by magical means the well-being of the dead. After Dynasty XVIII the practice of fitting a cartonnage case shaped to the form of the mummified body became steadily more common. These were painted with scenes previously found on inner coffins—the winged sun-disk or scarab beetle, under-world demons, deities in various attitudes, scenes of adoration and divine judgement, the sun-god passing through the underworld in his boat and the resurrection of Osiris (pl. 34). During the Roman period the decoration of mummies was often exceptionally elaborate with patterned bandaging or richly decorated cartonnage. The introduction of naturalistic plaster heads and 'mummy-portraits' make clear that the preservation of the individual personality was believed to depend intimately on the survival of facial features (*pl.* XI).

The embalmed viscera were placed in four *Canopic jars* (*pl.* 35), sometimes themselves contained in a special chest. The name is a misnomer devised by early Egyptologists who connected them with the Greek legend of Canopus, helmsman of Menelaus, buried at Canopus in the Delta and worshipped there in the form of a jar. Each jar was protected by one of the four sons of Horus: the human-headed Imsety, guardian of the liver; the ape-headed Hapy for the lungs; the jackal-headed Duamutef for the stomach and the hawk-headed Qebehsenuef for the intestines. The jars themselves were identified with the four protective goddesses Isis, Neith, Nephthys and Selkis. Until the end of Dynasty XVIII all four lids normally bore human heads and only thereafter was the distinction of heads customary.

Among a wide variety of other funerary equipment the magical servant figures or *shawabtis* are the most common (*pl.* 36). The original meaning of the Egyptian word variously written as *shawabti, shabti* and *ushabti* is obscure. The New Kingdom form *ushabti* may be rendered as 'answerer' in accord with their function of answering the daily call to forced labour in the place of the dead person.

34. Painted linen shroud depicting the deceased, a man named Nespatawi, as Osiris, flanked by attendant gods and symbols; Roman.
(Ht. 1.31 m; 1913.924).

33. Tamarisk-wood *cippus* of Horus: the god stands on a pair of crocodiles, under the protective mask of Bes, and holds various harmful creatures.
(Ht. 17.8 cm; 1874.279a).

Until the Middle Kingdom it was believed that menial work in the next world would be done for a wealthy man by the servants represented either in reliefs or pictures on his tomb walls or by wooden statuettes buried with him. Some time during the First Intermediate Period the idea emerged that forced labour was obligatory for every dead person, irrespective of rank. To avoid this the rich were provided with a mummified figure, usually of stone, wood or wax, inscribed with the owner's name and a magic formula. It was clearly intended that these figures should serve as substitutes for the dead at the morning roll-call for forced labour.

When the custom of burying wooden servant figures disappeared their function was transferred to the shawabti, which now became both a substitute for the dead man and a servant. The form of the figure changed and they no longer appeared singly. Made of baked clay, wood, stone or rarely metal they were shown carrying hoes, mattocks and baskets. The rich often had one worker for each day of the year and one foreman, with whip and flared skirt, for every ten workmen. Faience was first used for shawabtis in Dynasty XVIII and later became the most popular material almost to the exclusion of all others. Mass production in clay moulds lowered the quality of the modelling, but during Dynasty XXVI finely modelled

pieces were made again. Although rare Roman shawabti figures exist, the practice of using them virtually ceased at the end of the dynastic period.

During the Saïte period the shawabti text ran something as follows:

(Name of the Owner). He says 'Oh, Shawabti! If (owner's name) is called upon to do all the work which is obligatory for a man in the next world, to tear up weeds, you will say, Here am I. If you are called constantly for what must be done there to cultivate the fields, to water the river banks and to carry away the sand from the West to the East and vice versa, you will say, Here am I.' As this text shows the Egyptians believed that there would be a regular need in the hereafter for exactly the same tasks as followed the annual inundation in the Nile Valley.

In the Later Period another object becomes characteristic of burials. These *Ptah-Seker-Osiris figures*, commonly painted wood, associate in a single figure the characteristics of Ptah, god of creation, Seker, god of the necropolis, and Osiris, god of the underworld. Their bodies and bases were often made with cavities to hold fragments of the deceased's body or magical papyri.

Though museum visitors will rarely have the opportunity to study the development of Egyptian funerary architecture, they will constantly be presented with a

35. Set of four limestone canopic jars belonging to Djedbastetefankh, from his tomb at Hawara, Dynasty XXX; the lids depict, *left to right*, Hapy, Imsety, Qebehsenuef and Duamutef, the 'Four Sons of Horus'. (Ht.51 cm; 1889.1320-3).

36. Shawabtis of various owners and dates, *left to right:* Nakht, Overseer of the Delta in Dynasty XII, from his tomb at Abydos, carved in serpentine; a bearded foreigner of Dynasty XXI, faience; the lady Djymyra, painted limestone, Dynasty XVIII-XIX; the royal scribe Horkhebe, son of Khakhons, glassy faience, Dynasty XXV-VI; the priest of Neith, Horudja, born of Shedet, faience, Dynasty XXVI.
(Hts. 26.8, 3.05, 30.5, 16.0, 25.8 cm; E.2128, from tomb E.105, 1968.776, Queen's College Loan 13, 1879.269,1889.1072).

whole range of *funerary stelae*. The word, of Greek origin, means no more than a pillar or vertical tablet, often inscribed or decorated. From the earliest use of writing in Egypt they were placed in tombs, first perhaps only as identification of the owner, but rapidly as a vital aspect of its magico-religious furnishings. The persistent elements in a slowly developing range of monuments were the representations of the deceased, also maybe his family, and a variety of offerings with an hieroglyphic text through which all manner of offerings, privileges and benefits in the hereafter were invoked for the owner through the pharaoh and the appropriate deities. For the Egyptologist these objects have a rather different significance. Though often cryptic and stereotyped the inscriptions, ranging as they do through the aristocracy and administrative classes, provide invaluable information for the detailed reconstruction of ancient Egyptian society.

4. Nubia

The geographical relation of Egypt and Nubia has already been briefly considered (p. 6). Ironically the rapid development of archaeological exploration in Nubia since 1907 owes much to the Aswan dams, the first built in 1902, which have progressively flooded more and more ancient sites. In 1907-8, following a decision to increase the height of the Aswan dam, the first systematic archaeological survey of Nubia was undertaken by the American archaeologist Reisner, whose original analysis of the country's cultural history, the result of a single season's work, remains still the basic framework for study. In 1929-31 a second archaeological survey, under the English archaeologists Emery and Kirwan, followed proposals to raise the dam yet more. More recently intensive fieldwork preceded the creation of the new High Dam south of Aswan. The Ashmolean's Nubian collection comes largely from the excavations of the Oxford Expedition

Figure 3. Map of Nubia and the Sudan.

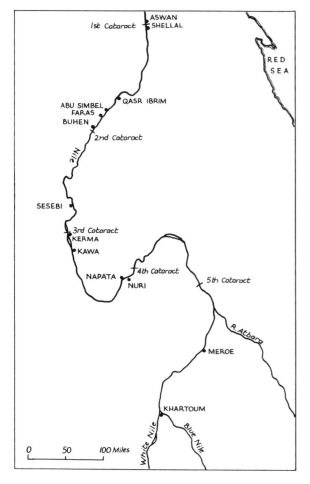

to Nubia in 1910-14 and 1929-34 under Griffith, and 1935-6 under Kirwan. Small collections of objects have come from more recent excavations by Emery at Buhen and Qasr Ibrim (*fig. 3*).

It was long thought that Nubia was a culturally backward region in the Late Palaeolithic period, but recent research has shown that it was participating in the fundamental changes that led to settled farming communities, as in Egypt (see p. 11). About 3100 B.C. people known as Reisner's 'A' Group established themselves in an area extending from south of the Second Cataract northwards to Shellal. Local red-polished plain pottery and red-and-black rippled wares predominate in association with Egyptian wares of very late pre- and protodynastic times. Although Nubia did not share in the cultural changes which marked the advent of dynastic Egypt, the rulers of Egypt soon realized the importance of the quarries and rich caravan trade through Nubia. Egyptian military intervention in Dynasty I, to protect trade with the south, may account for the disappearance of sedentary life in Lower Nubia about this time.

During the Old Kingdom Egypt was content with sporadic expeditions rather than any form of military occupation. By the First Intermediate Period Nubia was settled by a people, Reisner's 'C' Group,* whose distinctive black, incised pottery bowls are related to much earlier local pottery. These people were sedentary cattle-breeders, who buried the heads of cattle and goats in close proximity to their graves. Unlike the earlier A-Group tribes, those of the C-group did not become dependent on food imported from Egypt and thus vulnerable to Egyptian policies, nor did the rulers of the XIIth Dynasty seek to establish their authority by driving out the native inhabitants. In order to exploit the resources of the Eastern Desert they built an impressive series of forts to protect their frontier and lines of communication. The gradual waning of Egyptian power though the XIIIth dynasty opened the way for an unprecedented prosperity among the C-group tribes, with marked Egyptianizing traits in their material culture. A distinctive aspect of the C-peoples culture is represented by the so-called "Pan-Graves" (see p. 23) of the Second Intermediate period.

In Dynasty XVIII the re-occupation of Nubia marked a new and decisive stage in Egypt's relations with Nubia. The frontier of Egypt was extended to the south at a point upstream from the Fourth Cataract, towns and temples were built and Egyptian adminis-

*His B-group was mis-dated aspect of A-group.

37. Bronze mirror-cover decorated with the child Horus on a lotus, surrounded by birds and beasts, some of them mythological; from a tomb at Faras, 1st century B.C. – 1st century A.D. (Diam. 19.2 cm; 1912.460, from tomb 2589).

tration properly organized. No distinctive native culture of this period has yet been identified; C-Group survived into the XVIIIth Dynasty and was then submerged. Napata, just before the Fourth Cataract, became an important administrative centre on the effective southern frontier of Egyptian influence with a temple to Amun and a fully Egyptianized community. It was from this society that the first native ruling dynasty slowly emerged as the power of the central authority in Egypt progressively waned from *c.* 1050 B.C. From Napata, as we have seen (p. 31), an invasion of Egypt was started by Kashta in the middle of the eighth century B.C. which was to establish Dynasty XXV, or the Nubian Dynasty, in Egypt until, about a

century later, Assyrian invasions drove it back into Nubia. Then as cultural, economic and political links with Egypt declined, political authority passed from the region round Napata and Nuri to Meroe, near the Sixth Cataract, in the early sixth century B.C. This kingdom survived until the growth of Axumite power in the fourth century A.D. The culture of Meroe owed much to Egypt, particularly to Graeco-Roman Egypt (*pl.* 37), but strong local traditions and influences from Arabia and India to the east gave it a character entirely of its own. Until the third century B.C., and occasionally later, Egyptian was the main language for official inscriptions, but after the second century Meroitic came into use. This language is still not

38. Pottery jar painted in red and black with lion-masks and cobra-goddesses on lotus flowers, from a tomb at Faras, 1st-2nd century A.D. (Ht. 19.3 cm; 1912.410, from tomb 1090).

understood, though both the hieroglyphs and the later cursive script have been deciphered.

The Meroitic legacy passed in very modified form to peoples classified by Reisner as the 'X' Group, who occupied Lower Nubia as far south as Firka. Growing influence from Christian Egypt brought marked cultural changes culminating in the formal acceptance of Christianity about A.D. 543.

39. Bronze hanging lamp in the form of a dove, from a tomb at Firka, 'X'-group. (Length 14.5 cm; 1935.488, from tomb A 12).

Concise Topographical Index of Excavated Material from Egypt and Sudan in the Ashmolean Museum

EGYPT

Abadiya: (see under Hu).

Abydos: Amelineau, 1895-6; Petrie, 1899-1903; Garstang, 1900; Randall MacIver and Mace, 1900-1; Ayrton, Currelly and Weigall, 1904; Garstang, 1907-9; Ayrton and Loat, 1908-9; Peet, 1909-13; Petrie, 1921-2; Frankfort, 1925-6.

el-'Amarna: Petrie, 1891-2; Peet and Woolley, 1921-2; Newton and Griffith, 1923-5; Frankfort and Pendelbury, 1926-37.

el-'Amra: Randall MacIver and Mace, 1900-1.

'Aniba: Woolley and MacIver, 1907-10; Eckley-Cox, 1909-10.

Armant: Mond and Myers, 1927-37.

el-Awniyya: Garstang, 1901.

el-Badari: Brunton, 1922-5.

Bahnasa: Grenfell and Hunt, 1897-1907, Blackman and Johnson, 1909-10; Blackman, 1913-14.

el-Ballas: Quibell, 1895.

Beit Dawud Sahl: Garstang, 1901-2.

Beit Khallaf: Garstang, 1900-1.

Beni-Hasan: Garstang, 1902-4.

Dafana: Petrie, 1886.

Deir Rifa: Petrie, 1907.

Dendera: Petrie, 1898.

Diospolis Parva (see Hu).

Dishasha: Petrie, 1897.

Esna: Sayce and Garstang, 1904-5.

Fara'in: Seton-Williams and Charlesworth, 1968-9.

el-Faiyūm: Grenfell and Hunt, 1897-1907; Caton-Thompson, 1924-6.

Ghita: Petrie, 1906.

el-Girza: Wainwright, 1910-11.

el-Giza: Vyse, 1837 ('Campbell's Tomb'); Petrie, 1906-7.

Gumaiyima: Petrie, 1886.

'Gurob' (see Medinet Ghurab).

el-Hammamiya: Brunton, 1922-5; Caton-Thompson, 1924-5.

el-Haraga: Engelbach, 1913-14.

Hawara: Petrie, 1888-9; Petrie, 1911.

Heliopolis: Petrie, 1911-13.

Hierakonpolis: Quibell, 1895; Garstang and Jones, 1905-6.

Hu: Petrie, 1898-9.

Ihnasya: Petrie, 1903-4, Blackman and Jones, 1909-10.

el-Kab: Quibell, 1896-7; Sayce and Somers-Clarke, 1901-4; Sayce and Garstang, 1904-5.

Kafr Ammar: Petrie, 1912.

Kahun (see Lahun).

Karnak (see Thebes).

Koptos (see Qift).

el-Lahun: Petrie, 1889-91; Grenville and Hunt, 1901-2; Petrie, 1914, 1920-1.

Luxor (see Thebes).

el-Mahasna: Garstang, 1901; Ayrton and Loat, 1909.

Maidum: Petrie, 1890-1; Petrie, 1910.

el-Matmar: Brunton, 1930-1.

Mazghuna: Petrie, 1911.

Medinet Ghurab: Petrie, 1889; Loat, 1903-4; Brunton and Engelbach, 1920.

Meir: Blackman, 1912-13.

Memphis, Petrie, 1908-13.

el-Mustagidda: Brunton, 1928.

Nabesha: Petrie, 1886.

Naqada: Petrie, 1895; Garstang, 1904.

Naucratis: Petrie, 1884-5; Gardner, 1885-6, Hogarth, 1899, 1903.

Oxyrhynchus (see Bahnasa)

el-Quantara: Petrie and Griffith, 1887.

Qasr Ibrim: Emery, 1961-2.

Qaw el-Kebir: Brunton, 1922-5.

Qift: Petrie, 1893-4.

el-Raqaqna: Garstang, 1901-2.

el-Rataba: Petrie, 1906.

el-Riqqa: Engelbach, 1913.

Saft el-Hinna: Petrie 1906.

Saqqara: Davies, 1898-9; Barsanti, 1899-1900; Quibell, 1905-12; Emery, 1953-69.

Sararwa: Garstang, 1901-2.

Semaina: Petrie, 1898-9.

Serabit el-Khadim: Petrie, 1904-5.

el-Shaghamba: Petrie, 1906.

el-Sheikh Fadl: Grenfell and Hunt, 1902-3.

el-Sheik'Ibada: Johnson, 1913-14.

el-Shurufa: Petrie, 1902.

Sidmant: Petrie and Brunton, 1920-1.

Sinai: Petrie, 1904-5.

Suwa: Petrie, 1906.

Tanis: Grenfell and Hunt, 1901-2.

Tarkhan: Petrie, 1912-13.

Thebes; Mariette, 1858; 'Royal Cache', 1881; Naville, 1893-1908; Petrie and Quibell, 1896; Daressy, 1898; Legrain, 1899-1900; Carnarvon and Carter, 1907-11, 1923; Petrie, 1908-9; Davies, 1910; Bruyère, 1929.

Tukh-el-Qaramus: Naville and Griffith, 1887-8; Edgar, 1906.

Wadi Maghara: Petrie, 1903-4.

Tell el-Yahudiya: Chester and Eaton, 1870; Naville and Griffith, 1887-8; Petrie, 1906.

SUDAN

Buhen: Woolley and MacIver, 1909-10; Emery, 1962-3.

Faras: Griffith, 1910-12.

Firka: Kirwan, 1934-5.

Kawa: Griffith, 1929-31; Kirwan, 1935-6.

Kosha: Kirwan, 1934-5.

Meroe: Garstang, 1909-10, 1911-12.

Nuri: Reisner, 1916-18.

Sanam abu Dom: Griffith, 1912-13.

Sesebi: Blackman, 1936-7.

Select Bibliography

In English alone, to which this bibliography is restricted, the range of literature on ancient Egypt is already enormous. The following books, which may be obtained through a good public library, are no more than an introduction through which the reader should be able to explore deeper into the subject with relative case.

General

C. Aldred, *The Egyptians*, London, 1984.

J. R. Baines and J. Málek, *Atlas of Ancient Egypt*, Phaidon, Oxford, 1980.

J. R. Harris (ed.), *The Legacy of Egypt*, Oxford, 1971.

W. C. Hayes, *The Scepter of Egypt*, 2 vols., New York, 1953, 1959.

T. G. H. James (ed.), *An Introduction to Ancient Egypt*, British Museum, 1979.

W. J. Murnane, *The Penguin Guide to Ancient Egypt*, Harmondsworth, 1983.

J. Ruffle, *Heritage of the Pharaohs: an Introduction to Egyptian Archaeology*, Phaidon, Oxford, 1977.

J. A. Wilson, *The Burden of Egypt/The Culture of Ancient Egypt* Chicago, various cditions.

Introduction

1. *Egypt's Legacy and the Development of Egyptology*

P. A. Clayton, *The Rediscovery of Ancient Egypt*, London, 1982.

J. S. Curl, *The Egyptian Revival*, London, 1982.

W. R. Dawson, *Who was who in Egyptology*, London, 2nd ed., 1972.

E. Iversen, *The Myth of Egypt and its Hieroglyphs in European Tradition*, Copenhagen, 1961.

J. A. Wilson, *Signs and Wonders upon Pharaoh*, Chicago, 1964.

The Natural Setting

H. E. Hurst, *The Nile*, London, 1952.

H. Kees, *Ancient Egypt: a Cultural Topography*, London, 1961.

Prehistory and History

E. Baumgartel, *The Cultures of Prehistoric Egypt*, 2 vols., Oxford, 1955, 1966.

A. K. Bowman, *Egypt after the Pharaohs*, British Museum Publications, 1986.

K. W. Butzer, *Early Hydraulic Civilization in Egypt*, Chicago, 1976.

Cambridge Ancient History (3rd edition) I(1), 1970; I(2), 1971; II(1), 1973; II(2), 1975; III(1), 1982; *Plates* I and II, 1977; III, 1984.

C. Desroches-Noblecourt, *Tutankhamen*, London, 1963.

I. E. S. Edwards, *Tutankhamun: his tomb and treasures*, Metropolitan Museum of Art, New York, 1976.

W. B. Emery, *Archaic Egypt*, Pcnguin Books, 1961.

A. Gardiner, *Egypt of the Pharaohs*, Oxford, 1961.

M. A. Hoffman, *Egypt before the Pharaohs: the prehistoric foundations of Egyptian Civilization*, London, 1980.

T. G. H. James, *Pharaoh's People: scenes from life in imperial Egypt*, Oxford, 1985.

K. A. Kitchen, *The Third Intermediate Period in Egypt (1100-650, B.C.)*, Warminster, 1986.
> *Pharaoh Triumphant: the life and times of Rameses II*, Warminster, 1982 .

E . Riefstahl, *Thebes in the Time of Amunhotep III*, Norman, 1964.

B. G. Trigger and others, *Ancient Egypt: a social history*. Cambridge, 1983.

Aspects of Daily Life

1. *Architecture, Art and Crafts*

C. Aldred, *Akhenaten and Nefertiti*, Brooklyn Museum, New York, 1973.
> *Egyptian Art*, London, 1980.
> *Jewels of the Pharaohs*, London, 1971.

A. Badawy, *A History of Egyptian Architecture*, 3 vols., Giza, 1954; Berkeley, California, 1966-8.

H. Baker, *Furniture in the Ancient World*, London, 1966.

M. L. Bierbrier, *The Tomb-Builders of the Pharaohs*, London 1982.

J. Bourriau, *Umm el Ga'ab: Pottery from the Nile Valley before the Arab Conquest*, Fitzwilliam Museum, Cambridge, 1981.

E. Brovarski and others, *Egypt's Golden Age*, Boston Museum of Fine Arts, 1982.

S. Clarke and R. Engelbach, *Ancient Egyptian Masonry*, London, 1930.

H. G. Fischer, *Ancient Egyptian Calligraphy*, Metropolitan Museum of Art, New York, 1979.

T. G. H. James, *Egyptian Sculpture*, British Museum, 1983.

K. Lange and M. Hirmer, *Egypt: Architecture, Sculpture and Painting*, London, 1956.

B. Landström, *Ships of the Pharaohs, 4000 Years of Egyptian Shipbuilding*, London, 1970.

A. Lucas, *Ancient Egyptian Materials and Industries*, 4th ed., (revised J. R. Harris), London, 1962.

K. Michalowski, *The Art of Ancient Egypt*, London, 1969.

P. E. Newberry, *Scarabs*, Liverpool, 1906; reprinted.

W. H. Peck, *Drawings from Ancient Egypt*, London, 1978.

W. M. F. Petrie, *Amulets*, London, 1914.
> *Scarabs and Cylinders with Names*, London, 1917.
> *Tools and Weapons*, London, 1917.
> *Buttons and Design Scarabs*, London, 1925.
> *Measures*, London, 1926.
> *Objects of Daily Use*, London, 1927.

G. Robins, *Egyptian Painting and Relief*, Shire Publications, 1986.

H. Schäfer, *Principles of Egyptian Art*, Oxford, 1986.

A. F. Shore, *Portrait Painting from Roman Egypt*, British Museum, 1972.

W. S. Smith, *The Art and Architecture of Ancient Egypt*, London, 2nd edition, revised, 1981.

A *History of Egyptian Sculpture and Painting in the Old Kingdom*, 1946, reprinted Hackcr Art Books, New York, 1978.

K. Wessel, *Coptic Art*, London, 1965.

2. *Science and Medicine*

A. and E. Cockburn (eds.), *Mummies, Disease and Ancient Cultures*, Cambridge, 1980.

P. Ghalioungui, *The House of Life, Per Ankh: Magic and Medical Sciences in Ancient Egypt*, Amsterdam, 1973.

R. J. Gillings, *Mathematics in the Time of the Pharaohs*, 1975.

J. E. Harris and K. Weeks, *X-Raying the Pharaohs*, London, 1973.

J. E. Harris and E. F. Wente (eds.), *An X-Ray Atlas of the Royal Mummies*, Chicago, 1980.

0. Neugebauer, *The Exact Sciences in Antiquity*, Brown University Press, 1957.

3. *Language and Literature*

A. Gardiner, *Egyptian Grammar*, 3rd edition, revised, Oxford, 1957 .

M. Lichtheim, *Ancient Egyptian Literature*, 3 vols., London, 1973, 1976, 1980.

W. F. Simpson *et al.*, *The Literature of Ancient Egypt*, Yale, 1972.

E. G. Turner, *Greek Papyri: an introduction*, Oxford, 1968.

Religion and Funerary Customs

J. Černý, *Ancient Egyptian Religion*, London, 1952.

R. O. Faulkner (ed. C. Andrews), *The Ancient Egyptian Book of the Dead*, British Museum, 1983.

J. Hamilton-Paterson and C. Andrews, *Mummies: Death and Life in Ancient Egypt*, London, 1978.

G. Hart, *A Dictionary of Egyptian Gods and Goddesses*, London, 1986.

I. E. S. Edwards, *The Pyramids of Egypt*, Penguin Books, 1982

L. Hornung, *Conceptions of God in Ancient Egypt*, London, 1983.

W. M. F. Petrie, *Shabtis*, London, 1935.
Funeral Furniture and Stone Vases, London, 1937.

A. J. Spencer, *Death in Ancient Egypt*, Penguin Books, 1982.

Nubia

W. Y. Adams, *Nubia: corridor to Africa*, London, 1977.

P . Shinnie, *Meroe*, London, 1967.

B. Trigger, *Nubia and the Pharaohs*, London, 1976.

S. Wenig and others, *Africa in Antiquity*, The Brooklyn Museum, New York, 2 vols., 1978.

Acknowledgements

In preparing the original edition I was most grateful to Mr. R.W. Hamilton, then Keeper of the Ashmolean, and to Miss Janine Bourriau, then of the Griffith Institute, for reading and commenting on a draft of this booklet. I owed a special debt of gratitude to my former colleague Mrs. J. Crowfoot Payne and to Professor J.R. Harris, whose constant help, advice and kindly criticism had contributed so much not only to the booklet but also to the displays it was designed to explain. In revising the text I have benefited from the constructive criticisms of my colleague, Dr. Helen Whitehouse. The changes are not substantial, save in the Bibliography, and for the text as it stands I alone am to be held responsible. The drawings were undertaken by Mrs. Pat Jacobs and the photography by members of the Museum's Photographic Studio.